TAXING MUNICIPAL BOND INCOME

Publications of the
Bureau of Business and Economic Research
University of California

TAXING MUNICIPAL BOND INCOME

By

LYLE C. FITCH

UNIVERSITY OF CALIFORNIA PRESS

BERKELEY AND LOS ANGELES

1950

UNIVERSITY OF CALIFORNIA PRESS
BERKELEY AND LOS ANGELES
CALIFORNIA

❖

CAMBRIDGE UNIVERSITY PRESS
LONDON, ENGLAND

Preface

FEDERAL TAXATION *of the interest on state and local in-debtedness has been one of the most contentious of the issues arising out of the American federal-state relationship. For the most part, the contributors to the extensive literature and participants in the numerous discussions on the subject have been engaged either in attacking or defending the immunity and there has been relatively little exploration of the possibilities for a justifiable and mutually acceptable compromise. The main purpose of the present study is to establish a basis for such a compromise.*

For suggestions and criticism I am indebted to many people, of whom the following especially deserve mention: Professors Robert Murray Haig, Carl Shoup, Horace Taylor and Robert Eastwood, all of the Columbia University faculty, and Mr. Rollin Bennett. In the capacities of proofreader and critic, my wife, Violet Fitch, has given invaluable assistance. These people have contributed much to the study; for its deficiencies I assume sole responsibility.

L. C. F.

Contents

viiiContents

CHAPTERPAGE

eral Taxes Increased (State and Local Taxes Increased Correspondingly)—New Federal Borrowing or Outstanding Indebtedness Reduced (State and Local Taxes Increased Correspondingly)—State
and Local Tax-Financed Expenditures (Other than for Debt Service)
Reduced—Federal Taxes Reduced (State and Local Tax-Financed
Expenditures Reduced Correspondingly)—Federal Expenditures Reduced (State and Local Tax-Financed Expenditures Decreased Correspondingly)—Federal Borrowing or Outstanding Indebtedness Decreased (State and Local Tax-Financed Expenditures Decreased
Correspondingly)—States and Localities Reduce Borrowing—Quantitative Effect of Abolishing Exemption Upon State and Local Borrowing—Economics of Exemption-Induced Borrowing—Reduced
State and Local Borrowing and Possible Alternative Responses of the
Federal Government—Rate of Retirement of State and Local Indebtedness Reduced—State and Local Cash Surpluses Reduced—Conclusion

VI. Abolishing the Immunity from State Income
Taxes of Federal Bond Interest 74

Abolition of Federal Immunity as Compensation to States and Localities for Loss of Their Own Exemption—Fiscal Aspects of Abolishing Mutual Exemption—Impact on Local Government

PART THREE: TECHNIQUES FOR TAXING
MUNICIPAL BOND INTEREST

VII. Taxing Holders of Outstanding Bonds . . . 81

Suggested Approach—Outright Abolition of Exemption of Outstand-
ing Bonds—Arguments Against Abolishing Exemption on Outstanding Issues—Analysis of "Undue" Capital Loss from Outright Abolition
—Gain or Loss to Bondholders Selling Bonds After Abolition of
Exemption and before Redemption—Possibility of Refunding
"Undue" Capital Losses—A "Model" Tax on Present Holders—Principle of the "Model" Tax Formula—Computation of the Tax—
Treatment of Submarginal Bondholders—Determining Yield Differentials to Be Allowed—Comparison of "Model" Tax Formula with
Formula Employing Fixed Relative Differential—Other Comments
on the "Model" Tax—A "Model" Tax on Future Buyers of Outstand-
ing Securities—Problem of Capital Losses to Present Holders—The
Fixed Relative Differential Formula—Size of the Fixed Relative
Differential to Be Allowed—Treatment of Submarginal Bondholders—Other Advantages of the Fixed Relative Differential Formula—A Tax Credit of a Percentage of Bond Income

Contents

Tables

Part One

BENEFITS AND COSTS OF TAX EXEMPTION

CHAPTER I

Introduction

Few issues of taxation have been so hotly contested as the exemption from the federal income tax of the income derived from the obligations of states and their subdivisions. The issue was first debated in the Senate during the passage of the income tax provision of the revenue act of 1894,[1] when two amendments were proposed to exclude such income from the tax. The amendments were defeated and the act was passed without the exemption. In the Pollock decisions, handed down the following year, the Supreme Court held that the federal government could not constitutionally impose a tax on state and local bond interest; this decision has never been overruled.[2]

Subsequently, the question of whether the constitutional immunity established by the Pollock decisions would be abolished by the sixteenth amendment played a large part in the ratification of the amendment. To avoid further controversy over constitutional issues, Congress included a provision for exemption in the first income tax act under the new amendment and this provision has been repeated in every subsequent act.[3]

The exemption from taxation of state and local bond interest has been denounced by five successive administrations and on numerous occasions has been sharply debated in Congress. Its political significance is strikingly demonstrated by the fact that from 1927 to 1941, 101 resolutions for constitutional amendments to eliminate or modify the exemption were introduced in Congress; these constituted 14 per cent of all amendments introduced and more than twice as many as were proposed in connection with any other subject.[4] Probably no other measure was pressed so hard and consistently by the Roosevelt administration with so little success.

---

[1] For notes to chapter i, see page 137.

The duration and vehemence of the controversy cannot be ascribed to the potential importance of the tax as a revenue source—from that standpoint it has never been of great importance—but rather to the fact that the issue has become a *cause célèbre* in connection with three major social and economic controversies of the times: (1) the progressive income tax and the equitable distribution of income, (2) the issue of socialism versus private enterprise, and (3) the issue of centralized versus decentralized government.

As would be expected, the long-continued debate on the subject has produced a voluminous literature, much of it polemical. The major questions are fairly simple. On one hand, the opponents of exemption allege that it encourages uneconomic borrowing by states and localities and stress the fact that the present form of the exemption creates one of the largest loopholes in the progressive income tax structure, resulting in the loss to the federal government of considerable revenue. On the other hand, state and local government representatives claim that abolishing the exemption would increase considerably the cost of government at those levels and would impair the financial independence of state and local governments, thus undermining the whole federal system.

The last battle over exemption was fought in 1942, when the Treasury's proposal to abolish the exemption of both outstanding and future issues was defeated in the Senate after an extended debate. (See p. 55.) Since that time the Treasury has not raised the question. There is little doubt that it will be revived, since the basic problems, concerning which a great many opponents of exemption feel as strongly as ever, remain unsolved. Two of the widely discussed postwar tax plans, for example, advocate abolition of the exemption on all future state and local issues.[5]

In previous campaigns against exemption, the opposing forces have advocated outright abolition, which would eliminate both the tax loophole and the borrowing advantage of the states and their subdivisions; this method of direct assault has repeatedly failed because of the great political force of the united opposition of state and local officials. (See p. 54.) Before launching another all-out attack, opponents of exemption need to consider whether it is any more likely to succeed in the future. The following questions need to be examined:

1. Is the economic case for outright abolition sufficiently strong to justify pressing it even at the risk of continued defeat, or should a compromise solution be attempted?

2. What is the best compromise solution likely to be acceptable to both sides?

3. Should the attempt to abolish or modify exemption be confined to securities issued in the future or should it be extended to outstanding securities?

The purpose of the present study is to examine these questions from the standpoint of the economic and political considerations involved and, in the light of this analysis, to formulate a tax program which might serve as the theoretical basis, at least, for future legislative action.

The study is presented in three parts. Part One examines the market forces which determine the differential between the yields on tax-exempt and comparable taxable securities, the advantage or disadvantage to individual bondholders of purchasing tax-exempt bonds, and the advantage to state and local governments of issuing them. Part Two deals with the major objections to the present form of the exemption and discusses at some length the question of whether the fiscal system would be markedly improved by abolishing the present borrowing "subsidy" to states and localities. Part Three analyzes the technical problems involved in taxing outstanding and future securities and sets forth a suggested program based upon the preceding analysis.

CHAPTER II

Tax Exemption in the Market

THE IMMEDIATE benefit to state and local governments of issuing tax-exempt obligations depends upon the difference between the yield at which they are able to market their tax-exempt obligations and the yield which such obligations would command if they were taxable. The greater the yield differential, the greater is the benefit to issuing governments.

The advantage of tax exemption to a municipal bond purchaser[1] is established by a comparison of the taxes he is excused from paying with the yield he must forego by virtue of his investment in tax-exempt rather than taxable securities. This foregone yield or differential is the difference between the tax-exempt yield actually purchased and the yield obtainable by buying comparable taxable obligations (comparable, that is, as to risk and maturity). The less the differential, the greater is the benefit to tax-exempt bond-holders.[2]

FACTORS DETERMINING THE YIELD DIFFERENTIAL

In the past, when most government securities were allowed complete or partial tax exemption, the demand for (tax-exempt) government obligations presumably was conditioned by two factors, (1) the demand for tax exemption per se, and (2) the demand for safety and liquidity presumed to attach to most government securities, the latter depending upon (a) the preference of individual investors and (b) legal requirements relating to the investments of certain fiduciary institutions, such as life insurance companies, savings banks, sinking funds, etc. The importance of the safety and liquidity element in the yields of tax-exempt bonds presumably has been rendered negligible by the great supply of taxable federal obligations coming on the market since the policy of full taxation of new federal obligations was adopted in 1941.

---

[1] For notes to chapter ii, see pages 137–140.

THE MARGINAL ANALYSIS

In any case, the yield differential attributable to tax exemption per se arises solely out of the demand for tax-exempt securities on the part of purchasers who stand to gain, or at least not to lose, by buying them. Where the tax-exempt bonds are comparable with taxable bonds in all respects save tax exemption, any difference in yield must be due solely to exemption. The conventional analysis of the establishment of the yield differential runs about as follows:

Assume a simple schedule of progressive income tax rates, such as the following:

TAXABLE INCOME	MARGINAL TAX RATE
Under $10,000	0
10,000–20,000	0.20
20,000–30,000	0.40
30,000–40,000	0.60
Over 40,000	0.80

A potential bondbuyer whose taxable income exceeds $40,000 will be able to keep only 20 per cent of any additional taxable income. To such a bondholder, it makes no difference whether he buys taxable bonds yielding Y_t (letting Y_t represent the percentage yield on taxable bonds) or tax-exempt bonds yielding only one-fifth as much, or $0.2Y_t$. But anyone whose taxable income is less than $40,000 will gain by buying taxables to yield Y_t instead of tax-exempts yielding $0.2Y_t$ up to the point where his taxable income equals $40,000. Consequently, the demand for tax exempts yielding $0.2Y_t$ will come only from the group whose taxable incomes fall in the highest surtax bracket, and these will be indifferent about whether they buy tax exempts or taxables.

To tap the group whose taxable incomes range between $30,000 and $40,000, a yield of $0.4Y_t$ must be offered. Then, a potential bondbuyer can gain by buying taxables up to the point where his taxable income is $30,000, after which it is a matter of indifference whether he buys taxables or tax exempts up to the point where his taxable income exceeds $40,000. After that point, he will gain by buying tax exempts, since if he buys taxables, his return after tax is $0.2Y_t$, whereas by buying tax exempts he receives $0.4Y_t$. This differential will thus stimulate the demand of all potential bondbuyers whose taxable incomes fall in the highest surtax bracket.

Similarly, to tap the group whose taxable incomes fall in the third bracket, a yield of $0.6Y_t$ will have to be offered. In this case bondholders whose taxable incomes fall in the highest bracket will receive three times as much disposable income from tax exempts as from comparable taxables, and those in the second will receive twice as much; thus the demand of potential buyers in these brackets will be further stimulated.

The exempt yield will be established in the tax-rate bracket in which the net supply of funds forthcoming from individuals in that bracket and higher brackets, plus that from investors in lower brackets who buy for safety and liquidity, equals the demand of the issuing governments for funds.[3] Bondbuyers with taxable incomes in this bracket neither gain nor lose by purchasing tax exempts, other things being equal, and hence may be considered marginal bond buyers.[4]

This analysis applies only to undifferentiated markets. Actually, there may be different markets, with different demand and supply situations, for bonds of different grades and maturities, and for bonds issued by different jurisdictions. This is discussed at a later point.

MARKET FACTORS AFFECTING YIELD DIFFERENTIALS

The yield differentials resulting from tax exemption at any given time presumably depend upon a number of factors, both objective and subjective. The influence of some of them cannot be measured and there are only *a priori* grounds for thinking that they exist. The following appear to be most important:

1. The level of federal income tax rates applying to individuals and institutions who buy municipal bonds. Anticipations of changes in the level of rates also may be expected to have some influence.

2. The supply of tax-exempt bonds, relative to the supply of investment funds. This depends partly upon the following interrelated factors.

a. The level of the national income and the average propensity to consume.

b. The trend of the size of the federal debt and methods of financing federal deficits.

c. The net amount of new corporate financing.

d. The excess reserves of member banks and policies for controlling credit.

3. The distribution of investment funds between institutions and individuals who are in a position to profit from buying tax-exempt securities and those who are not. This will depend partly upon the distribution of income, the distribution of the control over savings as between taxable and nontaxable institutions, etc.

4. Conditions in the securities and commodities markets and anticipations of future trends. During upswings in the stock market, for example, wealthy investors may prefer to hold equities, particularly so far as their gains are subject to capital gains taxes at preferential rates. This may partly account for the fact that the proportion of tax-exempt bonds held by individuals did not change greatly during World War II, when income tax rates were very high and the supply of investment funds was large.[5]

5. The general awareness of investors of the possibility of escaping taxation through buying tax exempts.

6. The extent to which municipal bond buyers discount the possibility of the future abolition of exemption.

7. The degree of economic rationality governing transactions in securities markets and the degree of inertia on the part of investors who may hesitate to take the trouble to change their investments even when it might be to their advantage.

In addition, the following factors may be expected to affect the absolute, though not necessarily the relative, differentials on various bonds.

1. The general levels of interest rates. Other things being equal, when rates are high the difference between the yields of bonds of different qualities may be expected to be greater than when rates are low.

2. The stage of the business cycle—there seems to be a tendency for the relative spread between bonds of different qualities to increase during periods of recession and depression.[6]

Professor Lucile Derrick has recently finished an extensive analysis of the effects of tax exemption and related factors upon bond yields, in the course of which she investigated the influence of some of the factors affecting yield differentials between tax-exempt and taxable bonds.[7] Using a multiple correlation formula, in which average annual yield differentials between top-grade municipal and corporate bonds constituted the dependent variable,[8] she measured the influence of the following variables over the period 1919–1941 inclusive.

1. The level of surtax rates, as measured by a weighted average of supramarginal surtax rates.[9] This factor directly accounted for 35 per cent of the total variance of the yield differentials, and in combination with other factors helped account for another 10 per cent. This series, however, does not indicate the influence of anticipations of future tax-rate changes, which in some periods are probably a significant determinant of yield differentials.[10]

2. Annual amounts of new corporate flotations. This variable directly accounted for 4.5 per cent, and in combination with other variables helped account for another 10 per cent of the total variance in yield differentials.[11]

3. Amounts of tax-exempt securities outstanding, as measured by deviations of amounts actually outstanding each year from a trend curve fitted to the data. The influence of this factor turned out to be negligible.[12]

It seems to the writer that the use of a series representing absolute or relative changes in the amount of bonds outstanding ordinarily might be expected to yield more significant results than the series representing deviations from a trend curve, particularly if the series representing absolute or relative changes were used in connection with series representing such factors as the supply of investment funds and new corporate flotations. In the period covered by Professor Derrick's analysis (1919–1941), however, the influence of changes in the amount of tax exempts outstanding would be difficult to ascertain because there was very little change after 1931.

Considering these factors, it seems unwise to abandon the hypothesis that the supply of tax exempts outstanding may under some circumstances considerably affect yield differentials.

4. Stock prices, as measured by a common-stock price index. The influence of this factor proved to be negligible. The series used, of course, does not indicate anticipations of changes in the level of stock prices which would be an important factor in decisions to switch from tax exempts to stocks and vice versa.

In summary, the four variables examined by Professor Derrick accounted for about 61 per cent of the total variance in yield differentials, but most of this explained variation is attributed to only two of the variables—the level of surtax rates and the amounts of new corporate flotations.

The writer questions the adequacy of this correlation procedure, however, for reasons besides those already mentioned. The most important independent variable is the series of weighted supramarginal tax rates, which is used as a measure of the demand for exemption. The weights are the amounts of taxes paid by the income groups falling in the various surtax brackets. But the marginal tax bracket itself is defined by the differential between the taxable and tax-exempt yields; thus the size of the weighted supramarginal tax rate computed for any given year depends partly upon the size of the yield differential. The higher the yield differential, the higher will be the supramarginal tax rate; the correlation between these two variables, therefore, may be partly spurious. Second, adjustments to changes in the level of tax rates may take some time to effect as investors shift from taxables to tax exempts or vice versa, so that there will tend to be a lag between changes in tax rates and changes in relative yield differentials.

Third, the series of supramarginal tax rates does not reflect a large part of the total demand—that of corporate and institutional investors—nor does it reflect adequately the demand of individuals already holding blocks of tax-exempt securities. To take an extreme case, the demand of a wealthy individual receiving all his income from municipal bonds would not be reflected at all. Fourth, none of the variables used reflect the influence upon municipal yields of the supply of partially tax-exempt United States government securities. Finally, the only yields included are those of high-grade bonds.

An extensive analysis of yield differentials is beyond the scope of this study. Some of the problems of defining and measuring yield differentials are considered in the following paragraphs, however, and to get a general picture of the influence of tax exemption on the yields of top-grade bonds over the last three decades, several series of bond yields are compared.

The tax-exemption differential applying to the yield of a municipal bond at the time of sale may be defined in several different ways. Probably it is most conveniently thought of as the difference between the yield as computed from the sale price and the yield at which it would sell to be taxable, or, what amounts to approximately the same thing, the difference between the yield of a tax-exempt bond and that of a taxable bond similar in other respects, including risk, term to maturity, and coupon rate. (In estimating the gains or losses from buying a tax-exempt bond, however, it is easiest to assume that the alternative is to buy a taxable bond at par. If this is considered to be the alternative, the tax-exempt and taxable bond usually would not bear the same coupon. See the discussion in chapter iii.)

Yield differentials attributable to tax exemption can be measured only by comparing market yields of bonds similar in all respects save exemption, including the conditions under which they are marketed. The problem of comparison is complicated by the numerous factors which may affect yields, including risk, term to maturity, tax-exemption status, callability, sinking-fund provisions, and other special features. The influence of some of these factors can be eliminated by comparing the yields of "plain" bonds. Random variations and the influence of risk, however, can never be completely separated from the influence of tax exemption (this problem is discussed in a subsequent section). In practice, therefore, it is possible to estimate the effects of tax exemption only upon the yields of highest-grade bonds, where the risk factor is reduced to a minimum. Even here, the problem is not simple. Some of the difficulties which arise are noted in the following discussion.

The first problem relates to the conventional concept of yields. The yield of an interest-bearing bond, as ordinarily computed, is merely an "equalization rate" which equates promised future payments from the bond with the market price. Where short-term interest rates vary from long-term rates, however, the device is somewhat ambiguous. For illustration, a bond due in two years, promising two annual coupons of $20 plus $1,000 at maturity, is essentially a bundle of noninterest-bearing notes, one for $20 due in one year and one for $1,020 due in two years. Suppose that market rates are 1 per cent on one-year noninterest-bearing obligations and 2 per cent on two-year obligations. Theoretically, in arriving at a price, the first coupon should be discounted at 1 per cent and the second coupon plus the principal should be discounted at 2 per cent. The true yield, of course, would be less than 2 per cent. A similar bond promising two $40 coupons would have not only a different price but a different yield, since the first $40 payment which would be discounted at the lower rate is a larger proportion of the total payments promised. Theoretically, for bonds of any grade, maturity, and tax-exemption status there should be as many yields as coupon rates. This complicates the comparison of yields, at least at the theoretical level, since yields of bonds bearing different coupon rates are not strictly comparable. The problem is usually ignored in comparing bond yields, however, since there is no evidence that bonds are ever valued in the manner assumed by these theoretical considerations.[13]

Retail bond yields depend to some extent upon coupon rates, however. Medium- and long-term bonds bearing high-coupon rates and selling at premiums generally sell at higher yields than comparable low-coupon bonds. Yield differentials between tax-exempt bonds selling at a premium and taxable bonds bearing the same coupon rates but selling at lower prices, therefore, typically will be less than differentials between the yields of bonds with different coupon rates selling near par.[14]

In attempting to measure the effect of tax exemption upon municipal bond yields, an investigator may be seeking answers to several different questions, which have not always been clearly distinguished. These include the question of the quantitative advantage of exemption to borrowing jurisdictions and the advantage (or disadvantage) of exemption to various investors. The immediate advantage to a borrower of the exemption of a bond issue depends upon the difference between the terms at which the issue is sold at wholesale and the terms at which it would have sold to be taxable. (This of course does not take into account the broader advantages and disadvantages relating to the effect of exemption upon the borrower's financial policy, particularly with respect to amounts borrowed and the types of obligations issued.) The advantage (or disadvantage) of exemption to an investor buying a tax-exempt bond at retail depends upon the yield sacrificed by having bought the tax-exempt instead of a similar taxable bond. Since retail yields may differ considerably from the wholesale rates at which municipalities can borrow on similar obligations, this is an important distinction.

Estimating tax-exemption differentials is further complicated by the fact that the only taxable yields available for comparison with municipal yields have been those of corporate obligations and, since 1941, Treasury obligations.[15] Most bond purchasers in deciding between a taxable corporate or Treasury bond and a tax-exempt municipal presumably take into account factors other than exemption, such as risk and the desire for diversification. Even top-grade municipals and corporates, or top-grade municipals and fully taxable Treasuries, are not precisely comparable because of the different characteristics of the issuing organizations and because there tends to be a different market structure for each of these three types of bonds.

The effects of exemption, we have noted, can be estimated only by comparing the yields of top-quality bonds. By the rating of the market, the highest-quality bonds, other things being equal, are those with the lowest yields. The measurement of yields of highest-grade bonds, however, is not a simple statistical problem,[16] and the results may vary considerably depending upon the premises on which the measurement is based. In this chapter, two basically different types of series are compared, (1) arithmetic averages of yields of bonds rated Aaa by Moody's Investors' Service and (2) "basic" bonds yields derived by David Durand in studies for the National Bureau of Economic Research.[17]

Table I (p. 19) presents a comparison of arithmetic averages of the yields of top-grade long-term corporate and municipal bonds for the years 1919–1948 inclusive. It has been generally assumed that top-grade municipals have had a slightly higher credit rating than top-grade corporates, although this is difficult to demonstrate conclusively. Various industrial groups, however, at different times in the past have been preferred to other groups. Up to the early 1930's top-grade railroad bonds enjoyed a better credit rating in the bond market than public utility and industrial bonds; Moody's series of average yields of Aaa corporate bonds, for example, show consistently lower yields for railroad bonds in the period 1919–1929 inclusive; in the period 1930–1934 utility bonds were consistently lower than those of the other two groups, while after 1934, yields of industrial bonds were consistently lower.[18]

To obtain comparable yield averages, Professor Derrick, for the study referred to above, computed series of average yields using the yields of forty-one municipals rated Aaa by Moody's Investors' Service, and a like number of Aaa corporates, each of the municipals being matched with a corporate with respect to coupon rate and term to maturity. These series (shown in Appendix B) are the most extensive available of bonds matched as to coupons, maturities, and rating. The corporate series, however, includes railroad, utility, and industrial bonds.[19] Assuming that the credit rating of top-grade municipals generally has been a little better than that of the best corporates, a better measure of the influence of tax exemption could probably have been obtained by using only yields of bonds from the industrial group preferred in the market. The advantage of matching bonds by coupon and term to maturity, therefore, is offset by the inclusion of bonds from industrial groups whose credit rating, as evaluated by the market, was not of the highest.

Table I includes only average yields of highest-rated bonds. The corporate yields are annual averages of the monthly series of yields of Aaa bonds compiled by Moody's; in each year the average used was the lowest of the three groups—rails, utilities, and industrials, For the years 1937–1948, municipal yields are represented by Moody's series of yields of municipals rated Aaa (this series has been compiled only for years after 1936); for the period 1919–1936, the average municipal yields of Aaa municipals are those compiled by Professor Derrick. (The latter series was compiled only through 1941; for the years 1937–1941 it corresponds closely to the average yields of Aaa municipals compiled by Moody's.)[20]

Aside from discrepancies arising out of the methods of computing yield indexes and the difficulty of getting representative averages of yields of comparable bonds,[21] the differentials between the yields of highest-grade corporate and municipal bonds may be due to a number of factors. The principal factors are probably the safety and liquidity preference ordinarily attributed to top-grade municipals and tax exemption, but there are also other factors. Commercial banks are permitted to act as traders in municipals and may derive profit from trading operations as opposed to holding bonds for investment purposes. They may also buy local bond issues to further public relations or as a community service. It is possible also that municipals have been preferred over corporates because of the fact that municipals usually have been issued without the call feature, which protects investors against declines in interest rates until maturity.

Although in comparing corporate and municipal yields some allowance should be made for the influence of factors other than tax exemption, it is difficult to determine in any instance what the allowance should be. Data on the relation of yields of fully taxable government bonds to top-grade corporate yields are fragmentary and inconclusive. To get an idea of the relationship which has existed at various times in the past, a number of series were compared, of which the following are examples.

The Treasury's series of the yields of all fully taxable Treasury bonds, neither due nor callable for fifteen years,[22] was compared with Moody's series of high-grade industrial corporation yields. During the period for which data on Treasury bond yields were available (the fourth quarter of 1941 through 1948), Treasury bond yields ranged from approximately 1 to 11 per cent lower than corresponding corporate yields. A comparison of data on "basic yields" of corporate and taxable Treasury bonds of various terms to maturity, computed by David Durand and Willis J. Winn for the first quarters of the years 1943–1947,[23] shows that "basic yields" of Treasuries of fifteen and twenty years to maturity were from 4 to 8 per cent less than "basic yields" of corporate bonds. (It is generally thought that Treasuries rate slightly above top-grade municipals although there is some question on this point.) In the period 1900–1913 inclusive, before tax exemption became an effective factor, the yields of high-grade municipals (as represented by the Standard Statistics index of yields of fifteen high-grade municipals) were from approximately 5 to 23 per cent less than high-grade corporate yields (as represented by the Standard Statistics index of yields of 15 high-grade railroad bonds).[24]

These data apparently confirm the general belief that top-grade government bonds have been rated more highly than corporates; however, neither they nor other available data afford enough information to isolate the effects of tax exemption from those of other factors, particularly in the period 1919–1941. In setting up Table 1, therefore, no allowance was made for the influence of factors other than exemption. If we can assume that the municipal yields in the absence of exemption would never have exceeded the corporate yields, then the yield differentials are the maxima which may be attributed to tax exemption.

The figures in Column 4, Table 1, are the differentials between the average corporate yields and municipal yields. For our purposes, however, relative differentials are more useful than absolute differentials. The relation of tax-exempt to taxable yields may be expressed in a number of ways, for example, by the ratios of the yields, by expressing the yield differentials as relatives of the tax-exempt or the taxable yields, etc. (It is apparent that each of these expressions bears a fixed relation to each of the others, also that if two ratios of exempt to taxable yields are equal the relative differentials will be equal.)[25] In Column 5, differentials are expressed as relatives of tax-exempt yields; these figures indicate the magnitude of the percentage increase in the cost to municipalities of borrowing at rates corresponding to the taxable corporate yields (with the qualification that these yields are computed from retail, rather than wholesale, prices). They also represent the percentage increase in the yields which investors in municipals could have obtained by purchasing corporates. In Column 6, yield differentials are expressed as relatives of corporate yields. These figures represent the percentage of income assumed to have been sacrificed by investing in top-grade municipals instead of comparable taxable corporates in the various years; also they represent the marginal tax rates above which investors stood to gain by buying tax-exempt instead of taxable securities. These data may be compared with marginal personal income tax rates on the first net income bracket above $50,000 (Column 7) to determine the advantage to investors at that income level of buying top-grade tax exempts instead of taxable corporates.

The yield differentials in Columns 4, 5, and 6 presumably represent the maximum spread attributable to tax exemption; allowing for biases in the indexes it is probable that relative differentials owing to tax exemption were less in many years than the figures show.

The figures indicate that differentials between yields of these long-term top-grade obligations in the period 1921–1925 were in the neighborhood of 15 per cent of taxable yields. In the period 1926–1930 they approximated 10 per cent of taxable yields; the decline in yield differentials probably reflected an adjustment to decreased tax rates. In this period, at least, tax exemption was apparently of no great advantage to states and municipalities issuing top-grade obligations. During the middle 1930's differentials ranged from 15 to 25 per cent of taxable yields. After 1940 there began a sharp rise, culminating in the high levels reached in 1944–1946, when exemption apparently reduced the yields on top-grade obligations by well over 50 per cent.

The high differentials obtaining after 1939 can probably be explained by the following factors: (1) the great increase in the supply of investment funds; (2) the relative scarcity of tax-exempt bonds (one source of supply was shut off when the federal government in 1941 ceased issuing partially tax-exempt bonds, and the amount of state and local obligations held by the public declined by approximately $2.6 billion between June 30, 1941 and June 30, 1946);[26] the high levels of personal income tax rates; and the high excess profits taxes (the effective rates were 81 per cent in 1942–

TABLE 1

COMPARISON OF YIELDS OF HIGH-GRADE CORPORATE AND MUNICIPAL BONDS

(1) Year	(2) Corporate yields[a]	(3) Municipal yields[b]	(4) Maximum differentials attributed to tax exemption (2) − (3)	(5) Differentials, percentages of tax-exempt yields (4) ÷ (3)	(6) Differentials, percentages of taxable yields (4) ÷ (2)	(7) Tax rate on first net income bracket over $50,000
1919.....	5.23	4.20	1.03	25	20	32
1920.....	5.64	4.54	1.10	24	20	32
1921.....	5.42	4.70	0.72	15	13	32
1922.....	4.74	4.09	0.65	16	14	31
1923.....	4.86	4.05	0.81	20	17	31[c]
1924.....	4.78	4.00	0.78	20	16	24
1925.....	4.70	3.97	0.73	18	15	18
1926.....	4.53	3.98	0.55	14	12	18
1927.....	4.36	3.91	0.45	12	10	18
1928.....	4.40	3.92	0.48	12	11	18
1929.....	4.64	4.20	0.44	10	9	17
1930.....	4.50	3.97	0.53	13	12	18
1931.....	4.36	3.72	0.64	17	15	18
1932.....	4.61	3.96	0.65	16	14	31
1933.....	4.29	3.69	0.60	16	14	31
1934.....	3.92	3.20	0.72	23	18	34
1935.....	3.53	2.73	0.80	29	23	34
1936.....	3.03	2.57	0.46	18	15	35
1937.....	3.06	2.52	0.54	21	18	35
1938.....	2.85	2.25	0.60	27	21	35
1939.....	2.67	2.08	0.59	28	22	35
1940.....	2.44	1.83	0.61	33	25	48
1941.....	2.50	1.54	0.96	62	38	61
1942.....	2.57	1.66	0.91	55	35	d
1943.....	2.49	1.39	1.10	79	44	75
1944.....	2.57	1.16	1.41	122	55	78
1945.....	2.49	1.07	1.42	133	57	78
1946.....	2.44	1.10	1.34	122	55	71
1947.....	2.53	1.45	1.08	74	43	71
1948.....	2.71	1.87	0.84	45	31	68

[a] Figures are annual averages of monthly averages of Aaa corporate yields compiled by Moody's Investors' Service. For 1919–1929 inclusive, the yields are those of railroad bonds, for 1930–1934, of public utility bonds, and for 1935–1948, industrial bonds.

[b] Figures for 1919–1936 are averages of Aaa municipal yields compiled by Lucile Derrick. Figures for 1937–1948 are annual averages of monthly averages of Aaa municipal yields compiled by Moody's Investors' Service.

[c] The 1923 tax was reduced 25 per cent by credit or refund under the Revenue Act of 1924.

[d] The tax on 1942 income was cancelled. To the 1943 tax as determined was added any excess of 1942 over 1943 plus 25 per cent of the smaller of the two taxes (or the excess of the smaller of the two over $50, if less than 25 per cent).

1943 and 85.5 per cent in 1944–1945), which probably furnished
the incentive for the acquisitions of municipals by commercial
banks even at very high differentials.[27] Relative yield differentials
fell sharply in the latter part of 1946 and in 1947–1948, probably
reflecting the repeal of the excess profits tax, the decreases in
personal income tax rates and anticipations of further decreases,
and the increased supply of tax exempts which began coming on
the market (see Appendix A).

Since Treasury bonds presumably are closely comparable in
quality to top-grade municipals, a better picture of the effects of
tax exemption can probably be obtained by comparing yields of
fully taxable Treasury bonds and municipals. In this connection,
Durand and Winn, in their study of "basic yields" of bonds,
present data on "basic yields" of municipal and Treasury obligations for the first quarters of the years 1943–1947 inclusive.[28]
"Basic yields" are defined as the yields of high-grade bonds of
given maturities free from extraneous influences, which should
include most factors other than tax exemption. The basic yields
are derived by plotting the average yields of high-grade bonds for
the first quarter of each year by term to maturity on a scatter
diagram. Smoothed "basic yield curves" are drawn to describe
the relationship between yield and maturity of the lowest-yielding
bonds. The basic yields for bonds of various maturities are interpolated from these curves and hence do not represent actual prices
or quotations.[29]

There is some question of the representativeness of these data,
but they afford a useful check upon the results of comparing average corporate and municipal yields, particularly in view of the
different techniques used in deriving basic yields and average
yields. In Table 2, differentials between the basic yields of Treasuries and municipals of twenty years' term to maturity are
expressed as relatives of taxable (Treasury) yields. They are compared with corresponding differentials between Moody's Aaa municipal series and Moody's series of Aaa industrial yields.

It will be noted that in this period, relative differentials between
the yields shown by the two sets of data are fairly close and show
the same patterns of fluctuation. For some of the quarters, relative

differentials between basic yields are higher than those between
the corporate and municipal averages, which is contrary to what
would be expected. This is due primarily to the considerable differences in those periods between the basic municipal yields and

TABLE 2

Comparison of Differentials between Basic Yields of Treasuries and
Municipals and between Yields of Aaa Industrials and Municipals

	1943	1944	1945	1946	1947
Basic yields, first quarter[a]					
Twenty-year Treasuries[b]............	2.44	2.50	2.40	2.19	2.30
Twenty-year municipals...........	1.28	1.05	1.02	1.00	1.20
Differentials....................	1.16	1.45	1.38	1.19	1.10
Moody's series, first quarter[c]					
Aaa industrials...................	2.52	2.53	2.50	2.40	2.47
Aaa municipals..................	1.54	1.18	1.02	.96	1.40
Differentials....................	0.98	1.35	1.48	1.44	1.07
Differences, percentages of taxable yields					
between basic yields..............	48	58	58	54	48
between Moody indexes...........	40	53	60	60	43

[a] Durand and Winn, *op. cit.*, p. 14.
[b] Figures are based on yields of bonds not eligible for bank investment.
[c] Figures are averages of monthly series.

Moody's series of Aaa municipal yields, the differences being
relatively greater than those between the average corporate and
basic Treasury yields.

RELATION OF YIELD DIFFERENTIALS ON VARIOUS BONDS

The yields examined in the preceding section were those of long-
term highest-grade bonds. The effects of tax exemption on these
yields cannot be completely isolated, due to the impossibility of
obtaining tax-exempt and taxable bonds which in other respects
are precisely comparable. Nevertheless, the preceding compari-
sons, while limited, suggest that yield differentials owing to tax
exemption of highest-grade bonds can be estimated within fairly
narrow limits.

We now ask if tax exemption affects the yields of all bonds pro-
portionally, that is, if relative yield differentials attributable to
tax exemption tend to be uniform for all bonds at any given time.
It has been implicitly assumed in many discussions that at any
given time, relative differentials do tend to be uniform. Since the
advantage of exemption of any bond depends primarily upon the
levels of tax rates, there is probably an underlying tendency
toward uniformity, for funds seeking exemption will tend to
gravitate to the bonds on which yield differentials are relatively
lowest and away from bonds on which differentials are relatively
highest. The strength of the tendency depends upon the number
of investors who are concerned primarily with maximizing their
expected returns and in line with this objective are willing to shift
among bonds of different grades and maturities, the existence of a
common basis for determining comparability between tax-exempt
and taxable bonds, and the extent to which tax exempts are freely
marketed. Even in an almost perfect market, however, some variation would be expected among bonds of different terms to maturity
if investors anticipated changes in tax rates, and among bonds of
different grades (due to the fact that tax exemption will be considered less advantageous, the greater the risk of default of interest
payments).

Also, the forces which would be expected to create a tendency
toward uniform relative yield differentials may be impeded by
various market imperfections and the possible compartmentalization of markets for bonds of various grades and maturities and
bonds issued by different jurisdictions. The leading types of imperfections which may be expected are discussed in the following
paragraphs:

1) Relative differentials may vary among short- and long-term
obligations for two main reasons: (a) expectations of investors of
changes in the levels of tax rates and (b) the compartmentalization
of markets for bonds of different terms to maturity.

The differences usually observed between short-, medium- and
long-term interest rates have long been of great interest to economists and students of finance, and the forces determining the
relationship have been the subject of much speculation and

theorizing.[30] Here the concern is with factors affecting tax-exemption differentials between short and long yields of obligations of the same grade.

If the forces determining the yield-maturity pattern of tax-exempt bonds were entirely different from those determining the pattern of taxable bonds, there would be no reason to expect any consistency of yield differentials between tax-exempt and taxable bonds of different terms. It seems reasonable, however, to think that the pattern of relationship between yields and maturities is determined primarily in the taxable bond market, since the amount of taxable obligations outstanding far outweighs that of tax exempts, and that the yield-maturity pattern of tax exempts is closely tied to that of taxables.

Other things being equal, if there were a uniform tax rate which was not expected to change in the foreseeable future, differentials between the yields of tax-exempt and taxable obligations, both short- and long-term, would be established by the rate of the tax. The ratios between tax-exempt and taxable yields of comparable obligations would tend to equal $(1 - T)$, writing T for the tax rate, or, putting the relationship another way, the differentials between tax-exempt and taxable yields, expressed as percentages of the taxable yields, would tend to equal the tax rate.

If the tax rate were expected to rise (fall) in the future, however, differentials between long-taxable and tax-exempt yields should tend to be relatively greater (smaller) than those between short-taxable and tax-exempt yields. If investors are merely uncertain about the trend of the tax rate in the future, they may discount the advantage of tax exemption on long yields, in which case relative differentials between long yields will tend to be smaller than those between short yields.

Where income tax rates vary among different types of investors, and where rate structures are progressive, the factors determining yield differentials become more complex. Many large investors have distinct preferences for obligations of different terms, so that for these investors bonds of different terms are imperfect substitutes. It is possible, therefore, that the market for bonds of different terms may be dominated by different types of investors subject to different tax rates.[31]

On the other hand, given a yield-maturity structure of taxable obligations, funds seeking tax exemption should go to the markets where the ratios of tax-exempt to taxable yields are lowest, and away from the markets where they are highest. If there are sufficient arbitrage transactions of this nature, tax-exemption differentials will tend to be uniform. If tax rates are expected to rise (fall) in the future, however, relative differentials on short-term obligations may be smaller (larger) than those on long-term obligations.

TABLE 3

DIFFERENTIALS BETWEEN BASIC YIELDS OF TAXABLE TREASURY AND MUNICIPAL
OBLIGATIONS OF DIFFERENT TERMS; PERCENTAGES OF TAXABLE YIELDS[a]

Years to maturity	Relative differentials, first quarter				
	1943	1944	1945	1946	1947
1........................	33	56	61	51	36
2........................	44	60	67	51	40
3........................	49	61	69	50	43
5........................	54	63	70	51	45
8........................	54	63	69	49	44
10........................	50	63	67	46	42
15........................	50	..	63	57	48
20........................	48	58	58	54	48

[a] Computed from data on basic yields presented by Durand and Winn, op. cit., p. 14.

Unfortunately, there is little evidence available on the relation of relative yield differentials and bond maturities. An examination of the data compiled by Durand and Winn on basic yields of obligations of various terms to maturity throws some light on variations for a limited number of periods. Table 3 shows the differentials between the basic yields of Treasuries and municipals of various terms to maturity.

Basic yield data used in computing these relative differentials, as has been pointed out above, are not computed from actual prices or quotations, but are interpolated from smoothed curves describing the relationship between yield and maturity for lowest-yielding bonds. Hence the size of the differentials depends to a considerable extent upon the shapes of the Treasury and municipal basic-yield curves. This procedure may distort the pattern of differentials; in some maturity ranges, for example, basic-yield curves fall below the lowest yields. It is presumed that the differentials between taxable Treasuries and top-grade municipals are due chiefly to tax exemption; however, other factors may have been at work.

Subject to these qualifications, the above data apparently show an underlying tendency toward uniformity of yield differentials for obligations of various terms to maturity, at least on the level of top-grade bonds. In most of the years the differentials are of the same order of magnitude, and the differentials for obligations of different terms show the same pattern of fluctuations over the period, rising from 1943 to 1945 and falling thereafter.

The greatest variation from the mean is in the differential between one-year obligations in 1943 and 1947; however, computations of yields are subject to wide margins of error in this maturity range. For each of the first three years of the period, differentials tend to increase progressively from the one- to five-year terms, and then progressively decline. This probably reflects peculiarities of market conditions, the supply of municipals being very small in comparison with the large volume of Treasuries. There is no evidence of either compartmentalization of markets or anticipations of tax rate changes; however, the number of years covered is small and conditions in those years were abnormal.

2) Relative yield differentials owing to tax exemption also may vary between bonds of different grades.

In practice, it is probably impossible to estimate, even within broad limits, the effects of tax exemption upon the yields of lower-grade bonds. This is due to the fact that the "goodness" of a bond at any given time, as Macaulay and other writers have emphasized, is a slippery concept.[32] Theoretically, the risk premium in the yield of a bond should be determined by investors' estimates of the probability that future payments promised by the obligation will be met. The "goodness" of any two bonds which are similar in other respects can be said to be rated by the market as similar only if they sell at approximately the same yield. The only taxable bonds which can be compared with lower-grade municipals are lower-grade corporates, but there is no way of ascertaining at any given time the market's evaluation of the comparative "good-ness" of a lower-grade municipal and a lower-grade corporate, since the influence of tax exemption and of estimated risk and other extraneous factors are inextricably mingled.

Besides the evaluation of the market, the only bases for comparing qualities of different bonds are the ratings of the statistical services. That such ratings do not correspond to the market's

TABLE 4

COMPARISON OF AVERAGE YIELDS OF BAA RAILS,
INDUSTRIALS, AND MUNICIPALS[a]

Year	Yield averages		
	Railroad bonds	Industrial bonds	Municipal bonds
1937	5.75	4.25	3.49
1938	7.64	4.49	3.64
1939	6.13	4.25	3.32
1940	6.12	4.08	3.00
1941	5.50	3.65	2.60
1942	5.56	3.55	2.82
1943	4.78	3.38	2.20
1944	4.16	3.15	1.95
1945	3.51	2.95	1.90
1946	3.28	2.83	2.37
1947	3.63	2.92	2.37
1948	3.91	3.13	2.90

[a] Figures are annual averages of monthly series compiled by Moody's Investors' Service.

evaluation is evidenced by the considerable discrepancy between the yields of various types of lower-grade corporates. Reference to the average yields compiled by Moody's Investors' Service, for example, shows that in the period 1935–1948, average yields of industrials rated Baa were consistently lower than average yields of utilities rated Ba, rails rated A, and in some years, rails rated Aa. The discrepancy in the yields of bonds of given ratings is shown by Table 4, which lists average annual yields of rails, industrials, and municipals rated Baa by Moody's for the years 1937–1948 inclusive. In all but three of these years, the differentials between yields of Baa rails and industrials were greater than those between industrials and municipals.

In comparing the yields of top-grade bonds, it can be assumed that the market generally has rated top-grade municipals as high as or higher than top-grade corporates. No such assumption can be made with lower-grade bonds; we do not know, for example, whether in the absence of tax-exemption yields of Baa municipals at any given time would have been higher or lower than yields of Baa industrials or rails. For selected years, the ratios of yield differentials to taxable yields, based on Moody's series, are as follows:

Yield differentials	1937	1940	1945	1948
Between Baa rails and municipals......	39	51	46	26
Between Baa industrials and municipals..	18	26	35	7
Between Aaa industrials and municipals..	18	25	57	31

Assuming that in the earlier years, the credit rating of Baa municipals corresponded roughly to that of Baa industrials, tax exemption apparently had about the same influence upon Baa municipal yields as upon Aaa municipal yields. (A different conclusion is indicated, of course, if it is assumed that the credit rating of Baa municipals corresponded to that of Baa rails.) But what of the later years? Did the credit rating of Baa municipals decline relative to that of Baa industrials and rails, or did the demand for tax exemption of lower-grade bonds increase less than the demand for exemption of top-grade bonds? Unfortunately, these questions cannot be answered.

As with bonds of different maturities, funds seeking tax exemption at any given time may be expected to go into markets where exemption is cheapest, that is, where relative yield differentials are smallest. This would create a tendency for yield differentials to be uniform, the strength of the tendency depending on the number of investors who are willing to shift among bonds of different grades.

Because of the lack of any common basis for establishing comparability between lower-grade tax-exempt and taxable bonds, however, it is more difficult to ascertain the advantage of tax exemption of any given bond. This may limit the price which investors are willing to pay for exemption. There is also another reason for thinking that relative differentials between yields of lower-grade bonds ordinarily will be lower than those between top-grade bond yields. The greater the probability that future interest payments will not be met, the less important is tax exemption, since exemption is naturally of no advantage when payments are defaulted.

There is no reason to think that yield differentials applying to lower-grade bonds would be higher than those on high-grade bonds, unless the compartmentalization of the bond market should result in the differentials on high-grade bonds being determined by investors to whom tax exemption is relatively unimportant. There is no evidence of such a tendency, particularly in recent years.

In any case, the bulk of municipal securities have been high-grade, at least as rated by the statistical services.[33]

3) Relative yield differentials may also be affected by the restricted market for some municipal issues. Some issues are not widely known and tend to be marketed at prices which are out of line with their intrinsic qualities, as compared with securities actively traded on national exchanges. The market for such bonds may be restricted to a particular class of buyers, such as local banks, whose benefit from tax exemption may be considerably less than that of individual bondholders.

Some state and local securities are acquired and held by private institutions and sinking and trust funds administered by state and local governments which are more or less restricted by law or custom as to the particular issues they shall buy. In such cases, yield differentials may be determined with little reference to conditions in the bond market generally.

CHAPTER III

Gains and Losses from Tax Exemption

THE PRECEDING discussion is concerned with factors which may be expected to determine yield differentials in the market. The discussion following relates to the gains and losses accruing from tax exemption to individual and institutional bond-holders and to governments.

GAINS AND LOSSES TO BONDHOLDERS

The gain or loss to a bondholder who has purchased tax exempts at a given differential, relative to his position if he originally had purchased comparable taxables, depends upon (1) the price he pays for exemption when he makes the investment, (2) the tax savings realized during the period the investment is held, and (3) the capital gain or loss if the tax-exempt bonds are sold before redemption, relative to the capital gain or loss from selling comparable taxables.

"INVESTMENT-IN-EXEMPTION"

When a bondbuyer acquires a tax-exempt bond yielding less than a comparable taxable bond, he invests in exemption. The price paid for exemption is somewhat ambiguous, conceptually, and can be defined in several different ways. It depends primarily upon the yield differential between the tax-exempt bond and a comparable taxable bond.

By investing in tax-exempt securities, the yield on which is lower than comparable taxables, the bondbuyer sacrifices the income increments which could have been obtained by buying the latter. This represents an annual investment-in-exemption, so to speak, and the value of the total investment-in-exemption, as of the time the tax-exempt security is purchased, can be defined as the sum of the discounted values of the annual sacrifices. The computation of the annual sacrifices varies according to whether the tax-exempt

[29]

bonds are bought at par, at a discount, or at a premium, since in the last two cases the book value of a bond, under conventional accrual accounting practices, changes over the life of the bond as the premium or discount is amortized.

BONDS PURCHASED AT PAR

In this case the book value of the investment remains the same throughout the life of the bond and the coupon rate equals the yield. The bondholder has in effect tied up the amount of his original investment for the time he holds the bond; he receives each year a return equal to the principal multiplied by the coupon rate. But by keeping an equal amount invested in comparable taxable securities, at the taxable yield originally obtainable, the bondholder would receive a larger annual return. The annual sacrifice equals the difference between the actual tax exempt and the hypothetical taxable return. The premium paid for exemption, or the investment-in-exemption, may be regarded as the present value of a series of payments, equal to the annual sacrifices, extending over the life of the bond.[1]

The premium for exemption might also be regarded as the difference between the price at which the tax-exempt bond is actually purchased and the price at which it would be purchased to yield the corresponding taxable return. The amount of the premium defined this way is the same as that given by the other definition. This is a less useful way of looking at the matter, however. Suppose that the price of a bond to sell tax exempt is P_e, whereas its price to sell taxable is P_t. The investment-in-exemption would be said to equal $P_e - P_t$. But when a bondbuyer purchases a tax exempt for P_e, in effect, he obtains exemption on an income equal to that obtained from the sum of P_e invested at the taxable yield, since if he actually bought taxables, the difference between P_e and P_t presumably also would be invested.[2]

ASSUMPTIONS ON TERMS OF ALTERNATIVE INVESTMENTS IN TAXABLES

In computing the amounts of investments-in-exemption and tax savings to be derived therefrom, it is necessary to compare the results of given investments in exempt bonds with those of taxable

---

[1] For notes to chapter iii, see pages 140–145.

securities. Such a comparison involves the question of the terms at which taxable bonds might originally have been bought, that is, the coupon rate and discount or premium. The problem can be handled by adopting one of two conventions: it can be assumed either (1) that the bondholder's original alternative was to invest in the same bonds to be taxable instead of tax exempt or (2) that the alternative was to buy at par taxable bonds with a coupon rate corresponding to the taxable yield originally available. It is usually simpler, and probably equally satisfactory, to adopt the latter assumption. In practice, most prospective bondbuyers probably estimate tax savings to be gained from buying tax exempts on the basis of this assumption.[3]

Example 1. Assume that under prevailing market conditions, yield differentials between tax-exempt and comparable taxable securities are, on the average, 50 per cent of tax-exempt yields (or 33⅓ per cent of corresponding taxable yields), that is, that the marginal income tax rate of the marginal bondholder is 33⅓ per cent. (See p. 137, n. 25.)

Bondbuyer A invests $1,000 in 4 per cent tax-exempt bonds at par to yield 4 per cent. To see what A gives up and what he gains, it is necessary to consider what would happen if he took the alternative course of investing $1,000 in 6 per cent taxable bonds, identical in risk and maturity, to yield 6 per cent.

He sacrifices $20 a year by buying tax exempts. The total value of exemption depends upon the life of the bonds. Assume that they run five years. Then, at the time of the original purchase, the investment-in-exemption equals the sum of the discounted values of the annual sacrifices, discounted at the taxable yield, or $84.25.[4]

BONDS PURCHASED AT DISCOUNT OR PREMIUM

Where tax-exempt bonds are bought at par and it is assumed that the bondbuyer's alternative is to buy comparable taxables at par, defining the investment-in-exemption is fairly simple. The concept is more involved, however, where tax exempts are bought at a discount or premium.

The book value (i.e., the original cost plus the amortized discount or minus the amortized premium) of a single investment in tax exempts bought at a discount or premium changes over time at a rate defined by the tax-exempt yield. The book value of an equal original investment in taxables will either remain constant (if the bonds are bought at par) or change at a rate defined by the taxable yield. Hence, where there is a yield differential, the book values of a tax-exempt investment and a hypothetical alternative taxable investment will never be equal after the date of the original investment, or, practically speaking, after the initial dividend period. In effect, amortized bond discount constitutes additional investment—an increase in principal; similarly, amortized bond premium constitutes disinvestment.[5]

Consequently, where tax-exempt bonds are purchased at a discount or premium, the income sacrificed in any period (relative to the bondholder's hypothetical position assuming he originally had bought taxables) may be defined as the difference between the tax-exempt return on the current book value of the tax-exempt investment and the return on an equal amount invested at the taxable yield originally obtainable. The investment-in-exemption is the sum of the discounted values of the sacrifices over the remaining life of the bonds.[6]

In order to compare a bondholder's actual position with his hypothetical taxable position, it is assumed in the following examples that he buys dollar bonds, and fractions of dollar bonds. This assumption of relatively small bonds corresponds to reality with investments which are so large that the conventional thousand-dollar denomination is only a small fraction thereof.

Example 2. If bondholder A purchases securities of a given issue at a discount or premium, the book value of the original investment will increase or decrease over time. Assume that he invests $1,000 in 2 per cent tax-exempt bonds, redeemable in five years, to yield 6 per cent. The market price of a dollar bond corresponding to a 6 per cent yield is 0.8315,[7] so that $1,000 will buy 1,202.65 bonds. The return on the investment for the first year is $60.00; actually, the bonds pay a dividend at the end of the first year of $24.05, and the rest of the bond income consists of the amortization of the discount—$35.95. At the beginning of the second year, therefore, the value of the investment is $1,035.95. The income for the second year is 6 per cent of this amount, $62.16, the dividend is $24.05, and the amortized discount is $38.11. Similarly, the incomes for the third, fourth, and fifth years are $64.44, $66.87, and $69.44, respectively.

Assume, as in example 1, that the ratio of yield differentials to tax-exempt yields at the time of the original purchase is 0.50, so that A could have bought corresponding taxable bonds, at par, to yield 9 per cent. The return during the first year would be $90, so that he sacrifices $30 during the first year by having bought tax exempts. At the beginning of the second year, the book value of the taxable investment would be $1,000; however, it is desired to measure what A loses by keeping invested, not $1,000, but $1,035.95, the "actual" book value of the tax-exempt investment at the beginning of the second year. The return on this amount, at 9 per cent, is $93.23, and the income sacrifice equals $31.07. Similarly, the sacrifices for the remaining years are $32.22, $33.43, and $34.72, respectively. The value of these annual sacrifices at the time of the original investment, discounted at the taxable yield, is $124.80.

THE TAX SAVING

GROSS TAX SAVING

In return for buying exemption, the holder of an exempt bond is relieved of the necessity of paying taxes for which he would have been liable had he purchased a taxable bond. As a first approximation, for any given year i, the gross tax saving on a single investment equals (1) the book value of the investment multiplied by the taxable yield originally obtainable, multiplied by (2) the marginal tax rate which would be applicable to such an income.[8]

This formula is applicable if it is assumed that the income from an alternative taxable investment would be taxed like ordinary income and that the income from so-called tax-exempt bonds is completely exempt. Both of these assumptions may need qualifications under some conditions.

The marginal tax rate (T_i) for any tax-exempt bondholder has been defined as the tax rate applicable to the income the bondholder would receive (in addition to other taxable income) if the respective book values of all his tax-exempt investments were invested at the taxable yields originally obtainable on comparable taxable securities. (See p. 140, n. 1.) For bonds bought at par or at a premium, the marginal tax rate would be determined, as for any other marginal taxable income, by the surtax bracket or brackets into which the marginal income falls. But with taxable bonds bought at a discount, part of the return accrues as amortization of the discount, is not realized until the redemption of the bonds, and under present practices is treated as a taxable capital gain instead of ordinary taxable income. The amount paid for the bond is its cost for the purpose of determining gain or loss when it is redeemed or sold.[9] For high-income bondholders who have held their bonds long enough to take advantage of the long-term capital gains tax rate, this may have the effect of lowering the effective tax rate on the return from taxable bonds originally purchased at a discount. Moreover, the taxpayer is able to defer payment of the capital gains tax until his bond is redeemed or sold.

Capital gains realized from transactions in state and local bonds are taxable on the same basis as other capital gains by virtue of the Supreme Court's decision in Willcuts v. Bunn.[10] But in municipal bonds originally *issued* at a discount, the amount of the issuing discount which is amortized while the bond is held by any holder is not taxable.[11] This means that with municipal bonds bought at a discount, only that part of the return represented by (1) the coupon and (2) the amortization of the discount at which the bond was originally issued is wholly tax exempt. The remainder of the amortized discount is taxable at regular capital gains rates. Consequently, tax exemption is less important to individuals who buy municipals at a higher yield than the yield at which they were originally issued. During the past few years, however, few state and local bonds have sold at discounts owing to the low levels of bond yields generally, the increased market value of exemption, and the improved financial situation of most jurisdictions.

Bondholders who have purchased taxable bonds at a premium are allowed, since 1942, to amortize the premium over the life of the bond and to deduct the annual amortization from taxable income.[12] For bondholders taking this option the effect is that of a straight income tax upon the return from taxable bonds.

Before 1942, holders of exempt bonds were allowed to claim amortized premium as a loss when they sold their bonds (i.e., if the selling price was below the purchase price) or when the bonds were redeemed. This meant that the return from state and local bonds purchased at a premium not only was tax exempt but that it was in effect increased by the amount of tax saved by claiming amortized premium as a capital loss. Since 1942, municipal bond-holders, at the time of sale or redemption of their bonds, are required to deduct that part of the premium amortized since the date of purchase or since 1942, whichever is later, from the original purchase price to arrive at a cost basis for computing capital gains and losses. The effective return on municipals bought at a premium, however, is still completely exempt.[13]

In defining the gross tax savings resulting from the purchase of exempt securities, it is necessary to make some assumptions about the terms at which comparable taxable securities would have been bought, since the effective tax rate upon the income from such securities may vary according to the proportion of the income comprised by amortized discount. The simplest solution is to adopt the convention already suggested, that is, the assumption that the original alternative was to buy taxable securities at par. Under this assumption, the entire hypothetical taxable return would be taxed as ordinary income.

The capital gains tax upon taxable discount amortization accruing on tax-exempt bonds is definite and measurable and should always be taken into account. For any given year, the tax upon a single investment in "tax-exempt" bonds equals the capital gains tax rate which will ultimately be assessed multiplied by the taxable discount amortized in that year, or, more precisely, since the tax is deferred until the capital gain is actually realized, the tax for any given year equals the present value thereof. This amount should be deducted in computing the gross tax saving.[14]

NET TAX SAVING

The net tax saving on a single investment for any given year equals the gross tax saving minus the income sacrificed by having purchased tax-exempt bonds.[15]

If the gross tax saving equals the income sacrificed, the net tax saving is zero, and the bondholder neither gains nor loses by having purchased tax exempts. This is the case of the marginal bondholder.

Supramarginal bondholders, the villains of the piece, realize positive net tax savings, which are in effect private subsidies, equal to the gross tax savings minus the income sacrificed.

For submarginal bondholders, the income sacrificed exceeds the tax saving, and the submarginal bondholder loses the difference by having bought tax exempts. (For another concept of the marginal bondholder, see p. 42.)

Example 1, continued (see above, p. 31). A's annual return on a $1,000 taxable investment is assumed to be $60. Assume that his marginal income tax rate is 80 per cent. This rate applies to the $60 dividend which would be paid by taxable bonds. By buying tax-exempt instead of taxable securities A avoids the necessity of paying $48 in taxes; this is his annual gross tax saving. But to effect this saving he sacrifices $20 gross income. Thus his annual net tax saving is $28.

Example 2, continued (see above, p. 32). Assume that A is subject to a capital gains tax rate of 25 per cent at the time of redemption of his bonds. For the first year, his hypothetical taxable income would be $90, his tax $72, and his income net after tax $18. His actual income from his tax-exempt investment is $60.00; $24.05 of this is bond dividend and tax exempt, the remainder, $35.95, under current practices ultimately will be subject to a capital gains tax of $8.99, the "present" value of which is $6.37.[16] Thus his net tax saving for the year equals $35.63. Net tax savings for other years would be similarly calculated.

CHANGING VALUE OF EXEMPTION ON A SINGLE INVESTMENT

The tax-exempt and taxable yields, the yield differential, and the successive book values of the investment are determined for any single investment at the time the investment is made, except occasionally with callable bonds. (See pp. 41–42.) The hypothetical marginal tax rate, on the other hand, depends upon (1) the amount of the bondholder's actual taxable income, (2) the amount of the hypothetical taxable income he would receive by having originally bought taxables instead of tax exempts, and (3) the level of income tax rates. These factors may change from year to year. The gross tax saving for any bondholder varies directly with the size of the marginal tax rate and this affects the net tax saving. If tax rates rise, for example, previously marginal bondholders become supramarginal, some previously submarginal holders become marginal and supramarginal, etc. The only bondholders not affected are nontaxable institutions and bondholders in the lowest income brackets for whom the marginal tax rate, and hence the gross tax saving, is always zero.

For all save omniscient bondbuyers and those who expect to hold their bonds for only short periods it is clearly impossible to calculate accurately total gross savings at the time tax-exempt bonds are purchased. If the net value of exemption is the controlling factor, however, no bondbuyer will buy tax exempts unless the sum of the discounted values of the expected annual gross tax savings exceeds the initial investment-in-exemption.

ACCUMULATED VALUE OF EXEMPTION AT THE TIME OF REDEMPTION OF TAX-EXEMPT SECURITIES

If, at the time a single tax-exempt investment is redeemed, the accumulated value of gross tax savings exceeds the accumulated value of the income sacrificed over the period during which the investment was held, the bondholder can be accounted supramarginal for the period and will have realized a net gain from exemption equal to the difference. For marginal bondholders the accumulated value of the income sacrificed just equals the accumulated value of the gross tax savings, and for submarginal holders the income sacrificed exceeds gross tax savings.[17]

AMORTIZING PREMIUM PAID FOR EXEMPTION

The premium paid for tax exemption can be regarded as amortized by the gross tax savings realized. The time necessary for amortization depends upon the gross tax savings realized annually. The formula for the amortization time is complicated and there is no particular advantage in deriving it here. It is obvious, however, that if the average amount of the gross tax savings realized annually is fairly close to the average amount of the income sacrificed, the time required for amortization will be fairly close to the life of the bond from the time of purchase. For bondholders who are consistently supramarginal the amortization time will be less than the remaining life of their bonds, in other words, a supramarginal bondholder will recover his investment-in-exemption before his bonds are redeemed. If the yield differential existing at the time the bonds were purchased is relatively small, the investment may be amortized in a very short time, and if the yield differential is zero, the amortization time, of course, is zero.

Bondholders who are consistently submarginal will not recover the full amount of the premium paid for exemption by the time of redemption and nontaxable bondholders will never amortize any of it.

GAIN OR LOSS ON BONDS SOLD BEFORE REDEMPTION

If tax exempts are sold at the same yield as that at which they were purchased and if yield differentials remain unchanged, the gain or loss realized from holding tax exempts is calculated in the same way as if they were held to redemption. In this case, the gain or loss is equal to the accumulated value of the gross tax savings realized, minus the accumulated value of the income sacrificed by having bought tax exempts.

In most cases, however, owing to shifts in market yields there will be capital gains or losses in addition to amortized discount or premium.

In conventional accrual accounting practice, the over-all capital gain or loss on any bond sold before redemption is defined as the difference between the book value (the original cost plus the amortized discount or minus the amortized premium) and the price at which the bond is sold. On tax-exempt bonds purchased at a premium, federal tax requirements follow conventional accrual accounting practice—bondholders are required to deduct amortized premium from the orginal purchase price to arrive at a cost basis for computing capital gains and losses (with bonds purchased before 1942, only that part of the premium amortized since 1942 is required to be deducted). Capital gains and losses on bonds purchased at a discount, however, are defined as the difference between the selling price and the original purchase price (except that for bonds originally issued at a discount, the amount of the issuing discount amortized while the bonds are held by any purchaser is not taxable).

The accounting capital gain or loss accruing from the sale of a tax-exempt bond is easy to determine. However, it is desired to ascertain the gain or loss arising solely from the effects of tax exemption. The idea of capital gains and losses arising out of the changing value of tax exemption is familiar; in fact, one of the objections to tax-exempt securities is that the increasing market value of exemption often makes possible the realization of windfall capital gains. But the objectors have seldom, if ever, precisely defined such capital gains and corresponding capital losses. As a matter of fact, this concept, like that of gross and net tax savings, does not lend itself to precise definition except on the basis of somewhat arbitrary assumptions.

The principal difficulty is in comparing the bondholder's accounting gain or loss with that which he might have realized by disposing of comparable taxable securities. In the first place, the accounting capital gain or loss on comparable taxable securities would be affected by the terms—the coupon rate and discount or premium—at which such securities were purchased and sold. (The same difficulty arose in connection with the measurement of tax savings.) Again, the problem is most easily handled by assuming that the bondholder's original alternative was to buy comparable taxable securities at par.

The principal considerations involved in determining the net capital gain or loss from handling tax-exempt securities are demonstrated in the following examples.

Example 3. A invests $1,000 in 4 per cent tax-exempt bonds redeemable in five years, to yield 3 per cent. The corresponding price is $1.0458, so that he would obtain 956.21 dollar bonds. The prevailing ratio of yield differentials to tax-exempt yields is assumed to equal 1.0, so that the yield on comparable taxables is 6 per cent.

One year later the book value of the 956.21 bonds is $991.75. At this time, A sells the bonds to yield 1½ per cent. The corresponding price is 1.0964, hence the amount received is (956.21 × 1.0964) $1,048.35. A's accounting capital gain is the difference between the book value of the bonds and the sale price, or (1048.35 − 991.75) $56.60; this gain is fully taxable.[18]

a) Assume that the yield on comparable taxable bonds over the period remains unchanged at 6 per cent, that is, that the prevailing market ratio of yield differentials to tax-exempt yields has risen to 3.0, indicating that the market price of tax exemption has been bid up. Comparable taxable securities at the end of the year would sell at their book value and there would be no capital gains or losses. In this case, the accounting capital gain realized is net and is assignable to the increased value of tax-exemption.

b) Assume that there is a general shift in the yields of bonds of this particular maturity, so that the yield of taxable bonds falls commensurately with that of tax exempts. At the end of the first year, when A sells his tax-exempt bonds, the comparable taxable yield is 3 per cent. It is assumed that A's original alternative was to purchase 6 per cent bonds, redeemable in five years, at par; at the time of sale, the book value of each dollar taxable bond would be 1.000. It is desired to measure what A gains or loses by not selling comparable taxable bonds of the same book value as that of his tax-exempt investment ($991.75), or 991.75 taxable dollar bonds. The price of the taxable bonds to yield 3 per cent would be 1.1151; the total price of 991.75 bonds would be $1,105.94. Consequently, the accounting capital gain from selling taxables would amount to (1105.94 − 991.75) $114.19. By selling tax exempts A realizes an accounting capital gain of $56.60 but this is more than offset by the accounting capital gain from selling comparable taxables, so that he incurs a relative capital loss of (114.19 − 56.60) $57.59.[19]

Assume that A is subject to a marginal income tax rate of 80 per cent and a capital gains tax rate of 25 per cent. In the year that he holds the tax-exempt bonds he realizes $30 therefrom; alternatively, he would realize $60 from investing in comparable taxables. His gross tax saving is (60 × 0.80) $48; he sacrifices $30 income, so that his net tax saving is $18.

Under the conditions assumed in (a), above, A's relative capital gain is his accounting gain; this would be subject to a capital gains tax of 25 per cent, leaving $42.45. Thus his total advantage from having bought tax exempts instead of taxables equals (42.45 + 18.00) $60.45.

In (b), his accounting capital gain is again $56.60, which would be subject to the capital gains tax, leaving a net "actual" gain of $42.45. However, his hypothetical accounting gain from selling comparable taxables would be $114.19 minus tax, or $85.64. Consequently, he sustains a net relative capital loss of (85.64 − 42.45) $43.19. Subtracting from this the net tax saving leaves a net loss from having operated in tax exempts instead of taxables of (43.19 − 18.00) $25.19.

In summary, the relative capital gain or loss from selling tax exempts depends upon the extent to which the accounting capital gain or loss is offset by the hypothetical gain or loss from selling comparable taxables of an equal book value. This depends primarily upon the relationship of the shifts of the tax-exempt and taxable yields. There is no simple formula for ascertaining the relative gain or loss in terms of the shifts in yields and it is most easily found by applying the technique used above to individual cases.

It is now possible to sum up the total gain or loss resulting from the purchase of tax-exempt securities sold before redemption. It equals (1) the accumulated value of gross tax savings (2) minus the accumulated value of the income sacrificed (3) plus the relative capital gain or minus the relative capital loss adjusted for applicable capital gains taxes or capital loss tax credits.[20]

BONDS CALLABLE BEFORE MATURITY

It has been pointed out that this question would seldom arise since few callable municipal obligations have been issued in the past.[21] The usual practice is to compute the yield of callable bonds with reference to the maturity date if the bond is selling below its redemption value and with reference to the earliest call date if it is selling above its redemption value. In the latter case, the yield differential would be the difference between the tax-exempt yield

based on the call date, say m years from the date of purchase, and
the yield of a taxable bond comparable in risk and maturity redeemable in m years. If bonds are called earlier or later than was
originally expected the value of the investment-in-exemption and
the gross tax savings realized from exemption must be recomputed
on the basis of the changed redemption date.[22]

ECONOMIC SURPLUS ARISING FROM EXEMPTION

The differential subsidies realized by high-income bondholders
from holding tax exempts have often been compared to the economic phenomenon of consumer's surplus.[23] Actually, however,
economic surplus exists only when "A buyer makes a purchase for
a sum smaller than the greatest sum for which the buyer would
have been willing to make the purchase," or "whenever a seller
makes a sale for a sum greater than the least sum for which he
would have been willing to make the sale."[24] Marginal bondbuyers in this sense are those who would not purchase if the price
were slightly higher than that actually paid (no matter what the
differential subsidy involved), and marginal bondholders are those
who would sell if the price were slightly higher than that prevailing. Since bondbuyers and bondsellers may be influenced by other
conditions than yields, it is possible to have marginal buyers and
holders, thus defined, in all tax brackets. In fact, there is good
reason to think that this is so, since if the purchases of high-income
bondbuyers were governed solely by the rate of return, they would
have bought many more tax exempts in the past than they actually did buy. This has important implications for policy determination, since if the differential private subsidy, or net tax saving,
were confiscated, it is possible that some high-income bondholders might sell their bonds, even if they could realize no more
net disposable income by buying taxable securities.

THE AGGREGATE GAIN OR LOSS TO GOVERNMENTS
FROM TAX EXEMPTION

It has usually been assumed by opponents of exemption that the
aggregate saving to state and local governments arising out of
exemption is less than the aggregate loss to the federal govern-

ment by the amount of the aggregate tax savings, or subsidies, accruing to supramarginal bondholders. Actually, the loss to the federal government and the states and localities of the subsidies accruing to high-income bondholders has been offset by the advantage to the states and localities of the inelasticity of the demand for securities of certain nontaxable bondholders and bondholders in low income tax brackets. The existence of the yield differential makes it possible for the states and localities to charge such bondholders more for exempt bonds than for taxable bonds, even though they do not benefit from exemption. This costs the federal government little.[25]

The aggregate current gain to states and localities depends upon the yield differential prevailing at the time each issue currently outstanding was originally sold; the current loss to the federal government depends upon this consideration, also upon the distribution of municipal bonds, assuming they were taxable, and the level of personal and corporate income tax rates. To obtain an accurate picture of the aggregate net gain or loss to all governments concerned, it would be necessary to know, in addition, how much less states and localities would have borrowed at competitive taxable rates of interest. Consequently, it is extraordinarily difficult to measure the aggregate gain or loss resulting from exemption in a way that means anything.[26]

However, since the available evidence indicates that tax-exempt bonds, especially top-grade bonds, had little advantage over taxable bonds during the 1920's (see Table 1, p. 19), the result through the years of exempting these bonds has probably been a considerable net loss to all governments concerned. The differential apparently increased in the latter 1930's (see Table 1, p. 19); but we should note that the majority of state and local issues during the 1930's were refunding issues and taxing these might have prevented some bonds from being sold and put additional burdens on hard-pressed states and localities. (See Appendix A.)

In any case, measuring the net gain or loss to governments from exemption is something like measuring the wages of sin. The point is that high-income bondholders get differential subsidies, and to the extent that such subsidies are not financed by governments they must be financed by submarginal bondholders—there is no escaping this conclusion. As Simons says,"It is the main purpose of the income tax to secure an equitable, progressive distribution of tax burdens among individuals,"[27] and ". . . one may well reverse Hardy's implication and assert that the results of the policy would probably be less objectionable, on any reasonable welfare criteria, if it showed a heavy fiscal loss than if no loss or a gain were involved. Heavy loss would be indicative of a more uniform scaling-down of the burdens on persons of large income; while the absence of loss implies gross discrimination among such persons and a heavy regressive burden on other groups as well."[28]

The future advantage to states and localities of continuing exemption depends upon the extent to which the large yield differentials emerging during the war will be maintained. In 1945 the yield differential on top-grade bonds was in the neighborhood of 150 per cent of the tax-exempt yield; during the latter part of 1946 the relative differential began a sharp decline, probably reflecting the increased volume of new state and local borrowing as well as anticipations of decreased income tax rates. In 1948 the yield differential apparently declined to less than 50 per cent of the tax-exempt yield, and was lower than any year since 1939. (See Table 1, p. 19.) It is probable that the expected increased rate of state and local borrowing, coupled with some decreases in federal income tax rates, will decrease this differential still further, possibly to the level of the middle 1930's.[29] The opportunity for state and local governments to exploit the demand for safety and liquidity will be considerably narrower, moreover, because of the ample supply of taxable federal issues.

The further the differential falls, the greater will be the advantage to high-income investors. The advantage may be increased by buying exempt bonds on margin, with loans on which the note is less than the yield of the bond. The writer has been told of cases where wealthy persons have, through this device, obtained tax-exempt returns as high as 10 per cent on their own money.

Part Two

THE CASE AGAINST EXEMPTION AND THE QUESTION OF POLICY

CHAPTER IV

Major Objections to Exemption

THERE ARE two major categories of objections to tax exemption. Objections in the first category center on the advantage to individual (and, occasionally, corporate) bondholders arising out of the progressive income tax structure; and, conversely, the loss to nontaxable institutions and to individuals with low incomes who buy municipal bonds for their presumed liquidity and safety. The second category of objections centers upon the alleged misallocation of resources resulting from the ability of the states and localities to borrow at preferential rates of interest.

The campaigns against tax exemption in the 1920's emphasized both categories of objections. At that time the charge that exemption diverted capital from productive private industry and aided socialization was pressed chiefly by business organizations, led by the public utility interests, whereas economists focused their opposition upon the undue advantage of exemption to the rich and the damage to the progressive income tax principle.[1] In the most recent campaigns (in the late 1930's and early 1940's) the opposition emphasized the tax loophole and largely ignored the issue of misallocation of resources. This was probably due partly to the fact that by this time conservative business interests were more worried about "socialism" at the federal than at the municipal level, and partly to a desire on the part of the opponents of exemption to mollify state and local government representatives, whose vociferous hostility contrasted sharply with their apathy in the earlier period.

The major campaigns against exemption have concentrated upon its outright abolition and most of the literature has been either pro or anti. Consequently, there have been few attempts to make a balanced appraisal of the various issues considered by

---

[1] For notes to chapter iv see pages 145–146.

themselves. This is particularly true of the borrowing advantage which exemption gives to the state and local governments. The continued deadlock indicates the need for a reëxamination of the question with a view to finding a compromise which might be acceptable to the jealous exponents of state and local independence without sacrificing the principles of the economists. Such a reexamination is the main purpose of Part Two.

OBJECTIONS TO BENEFITS CONFERRED ON BONDHOLDERS

The principal complaint concerns the undesirability of maintaining exemption at the expense of granting private subsidies (net tax savings) to high-income bondholders. The value of the subsidy increases with the size of the bondholder's income; when the national income rises, for example, the taxable income of some bondholders may also rise, thus pushing them into higher income brackets and increasing the value of the exemption to them. The value of the subsidy increases also when tax rates rise, thereby increasing the excess returns to bondholders who bought when rates were lower and exemption correspondingly cheap. On the other hand, bondholders who buy when tax rates are high lose if rates decline. As Simons says, ". . . this device of avoidance is highly attractive only to the idle, passive holders of highly conservative investments,"[2] and also "it means gross differentiation within the upper brackets in favor of coupon clippers and against those actively engaged in business enterprise . . ."[3]

The private subsidies to the "idle, passive holders of highly conservative investments" accrue in part at the expense of nontaxable bondholders and small income bondholders, who lose more than they gain through exemption.[4] However, this objection probably was more relevant before exemption of federal bond interest was completely abolished.

In addition to the first principal objection, there are several corollaries.

2. The yield of the federal income tax is undermined, causing either decreased federal expenditures or resort to less equitable federal taxes.[5]

3. By allowing wealthy taxpayers a tax-free haven, exemption discourages them from risking their funds in investment in productive enterprise; in other words, wealthy individuals who now buy tax exempts might be so dissatisfied with the low net returns on "safe" taxable investments that they would turn to risk ventures to increase their incomes. This seems debatable, however, since there are some conflicting tendencies.

First, the high income tax rates which make exemption attractive may deter wealthy persons from risking their money in risky ventures. If there were no exempt bonds, these people might elect to buy safe, though taxable, governments, or they might even elect to hold their funds idle.

Second, if wealthy persons can put a part of their fortunes into tax exempts, thereby assuring to themselves a reasonably safe income, they may be more willing to risk the remainder. In any event, it is charged that the benefits of exemption accrue to "idle, passive, holders of highly conservative investments." Cutting off the subsidies to these people may be highly desirable, but there seems no reason to expect that such action will change their basic investment policies.

However, the available evidence indicates that the amount of funds diverted from private investment by exemption in the past, as measured by the exempt securities held by wealthy individuals, is relatively small.[6]

4. Maintaining such a glaring loophole for the idle and conservative rich creates social unrest and undermines the morale of the ordinary taxpayer. This is probably correct, although it may be questioned how many ordinary taxpayers understand the principle involved. On the other hand, some social unrest has doubtless been stirred up by the charge that abolishing exemption would impair the financial capacity of the states and their subdivisions. For example, teachers' organizations have repeatedly protested against abolishing exemption.[7]

The strongest objections in this category seem to be those concerned with the inherent unfairness of the system of private subsidies. The proportionately largest subsidies go to bondholders in the highest income tax brackets, which is contrary to the principle of progressive income taxation. Technically, not all the subsidies (net tax savings) are economic surplus, since some investors undoubtedly must be paid high returns to induce them to buy and hold municipals. Nevertheless, the regressiveness of the system and the general damage to the progressive income structure appears to outweigh any opposing consideration. This is generally admitted even by the ardent proponents of exemption, who generally confine their rebuttals to arguing that the evil has never been quantitatively great and to pointing out that other violations of the progressive principle are tolerated in the tax structure. The first point is questionable, even granting the validity of the statistics which have been produced to support it.[8] The second point is merely an attempt to cover up one evil by pointing to another. On net balance, the federal government has probably lost considerably more through tax exemption than the state and local governments have gained, but even if this were not so, most economists would probably agree with Professor Simons' following comment, "The problem of tax-exempt securities is perhaps largely illusory, *unless* one happens to be interested in the income tax as a means for reaching persons equitably and progressively; but from that viewpoint it is terribly real."[9]

OBJECTIONS TO CHEAP MUNICIPAL BORROWING

The case against tax-exemption benefits to the states and localities is less clear. For the most part, arguments against "subsidizing" state and local borrowing have been developed, as in the 1920's, by business groups, notably the utility interests, seeking to impede competition by state and local governments for funds, or by economists to bolster the objections against subsidizing individual bondholders. There are two main arguments. First, it is claimed that the preferential interest rate encourages uneconomic state and local borrowing and misallocation of resources. Second, opponents of exemption argue that the benefits which states and localities realize from exemption are in reality erratic and inefficient subsidies from the federal government and that if subsidies are to be granted they should be allocated on a more scientific basis. The first argument will be examined later (pp. 68–70). In support of the second, five points are made[10] in the following paragraphs.

1. The advantage can be realized only by borrowing, but this advantage is not available to those governments most in need of assistance, that is, those whose credit standing is relatively poor. The greatest advantage goes to governments with the heaviest indebtedness, which are likely to be the richest.

This contention is not altogether true because so far as yield differentials owing to tax exemption tend to be proportional to tax-exempt yields, the interest saving on a given amount of funds borrowed tends to be greater for governments with lower credit ratings. (Cf. pp. 62–63; also the comment on the objections noted in the next paragraph. Moreover, it is not generally true that the richest governments have the heaviest debts relative to income or wealth.[11]

2. The financial advantage to the states and localities with low credit standings is disproportionately expensive to the federal government. The argument here is demonstrated by the following example: Assume that city A, with a good credit rating, can sell bonds at 3 per cent, and city B, with a poor credit rating, must pay 6 per cent. Then for every thousand dollars borrowed by city A, the federal government loses thirty dollars from its tax base, whereas for every thousand borrowed by city B, the loss is sixty dollars.

There is a reasonable presumption, however, that yield differentials tend to be at least roughly proportional to tax-exempt yields at any given time. Suppose that the prevailing ratio of differentials to exempt yields is 0.5. Then, if exemption were abolished, city A would have to pay 4½ per cent, and city B would have to pay 9 per cent. Consequently, the real losses to the federal government's tax base per thousand dollars borrowed are forty-five dollars and ninety dollars respectively. This seems to bear out the previous argument. But what the argument overlooks is that the saving per thousand dollars borrowed is thirty dollars for city B and only fifteen for city A, so that the benefit extended by the exemption tends to be proportional to the loss to the federal government.

3. The financial advantage is available only to jurisdictions which resort to borrowing and therefore must be expected to stimulate borrowing in preference to taxation, thus distorting decisions on questions of state or local financial policy.

This implies that exemption induces states and localities to finance some activities by borrowing which they would otherwise finance through taxation. It is questionable whether the preferential interest rate would not have more of a tendency to stimulate total spending. However, it does not necessarily follow that decisions on questions of financial policy are always "distorted," in the invidious sense, where the exemption causes borrowing to be substituted for taxation. The logical premise of this objection is that state and local authorities can arrive at "undistorted" decisions whether to tax or borrow only by proceeding on the basis of what they would do if their bonds were not exempt. It would seem that such decisions should be taken with respect to various other factors as well, such as the phase of the business cycle, integrating fiscal policy with that of the federal government and other states and localities, and the financial condition of the particular jurisdiction concerned; and that exemption may at times encourage action which from these points of view is economically beneficial.

4. The financial advantage flowing from exemption is highly uncertain because it rests upon the willingness of investors to pay for an uncertain advantage (which will be affected in the future by changing tax rates). That is, the price of tax-exempt bonds is presumably affected by anticipations of future federal tax rates. Since this is an uncertain factor, the bond purchaser must discount the risk involved.

There is no question but that the financial advantage is uncertain; however, it is improbable that this always works to the disadvantage of the states and localities. On some occasions, investors may anticipate increased tax rates and be willing to pay correspondingly high premiums for exemption.

5. The advantage to the states and localities is determined by decisions on grounds unrelated to the desirability of varying the value of federal assistance, being determined in large part by the level of federal income tax rates.

This undoubtedly constitutes a real objection to the exemption viewed as a device for distributing federal subsidies, compared with other possible formulas. (See p. 73.) However, there are also worse subsidies. (See p. 70.) And the fact that some of the other objections to the exemption as a subsidy device appear to have less force than has been claimed for them raises the question of whether the "subsidy" is as bad as its opponents think.

In addition, there is a question as to the point of view involved in regarding the exemption as a subsidy, which is that of a federal fiscal authority attempting to decide upon the most desirable subsidy formula. If tax exemption had never existed and if the federal government were merely considering possible techniques for allocating a given amount of federal funds to states and their subdivisions, undoubtedly a better formula could be found. However, these are not the conditions of the problem. Tax exemption has existed since the inauguration of the federal income tax under the sixteenth amendment, has been an integral part of the federal-state-local tax structure, and doubtless has conditioned to some extent the development of the structure. Many present municipal financial arrangements have been predicated upon its continuation. (See p. 147, n. 14.) At the same time, the case against private subsidies to high-income bondholders appears unassailable and few voices have been raised in its defense save to deny that the evil is quantitatively great. What is needed is a reëxamination of the question to see whether there are grounds for abolishing the subsidy to the upper income bondholders while preserving the exemption benefit, or part of the exemption benefit, to states and localities, assuming that such an arrangement would be practicable.

State and Local Opposition to Abolishing Exemption

Recent experience indicates that pressure from states and localities may be strong enough in the future, as it has been in the past, to prevent the abolition of their borrowing advantage. Even in the early 1920's, when economic and conservative business opinion was almost solidly arrayed against exemption, when state and local opposition was lacking or relatively weak, and when states and localities were deriving relatively little benefit from exemption, Congress refused to go so far as to submit to the decision of the states a constitutional amendment providing for reciprocal nondiscriminatory taxation of government bond interest and the salaries of public officials. Presidents Harding, Coolidge, and Hoover all urged abolishing exemption, without results.[12]

During the latter part of the 1920's, public interest in the question largely subsided. Agitation against exemption mounted again early in the 1930's as a result of the growing national debt and rising tax rates. Several attempts were made by influential Congressmen to abolish exemption and the Senate in 1933 went so far as to accept an amendment to the National Industrial Recovery Act providing for the taxation of income from obligations of the federal government and its possessions, as well as state and local government obligations.[13] This amendment was dropped by the Conference Committee.[14]

President Roosevelt took up the fight in a message to Congress, June 19, 1935, recommending the "submission and ratification of a Constitutional Amendment whereby the Federal Government will be permitted to tax the income on subsequently issued State and local securities and likewise for the taxation by state and local governments of future issues of Federal Securities."[15]

Although a great many resolutions for amending the Constitution were introduced by various members of Congress, no further step of any consequence was taken until 1938 when the President in a special message to the Congress on April 25, recommended legislation to abolish income tax exemptions on future issues of municipal and federal bonds, recent Court decisions having indicated the possibility that this could be achieved without a constitutional amendment.[16] Pursuant to this recommendation, the Senate passed a resolution establishing a Special Committee on the taxation of governmental securities and salaries, which held hearings in January and February of 1939.[17] Hearings were also held before the House Ways and Means Committee in June and July of that year.[18]

The states and localities, which as a special interest group had not opposed earlier attempts to tax bonds, now brought tremendous pressure to bear. The Conference on State Defense was organized to fight the President's proposal on behalf of the states and municipalities and carried on an extensive research and propaganda campaign. In the hearings before the Special Senate Committee active opposition was expressed by the attorneys general of more than 40 of the states, by the Municipal Finance Officers Association, the United States Conference of Mayors, municipal leagues in 23 states, representing more than 4,800 municipalities, and other organizations speaking for state and local governments, as well as many state and city officers speaking for their respective jurisdictions.[19] Similar opposition was expressed before the Ways and Means Committee.[20] Nevertheless, the Special Senate Committee reported favorably on the proposal and it was endorsed by the Democratic party campaign platform in 1940.[21] After all this, the proposal was defeated in the Senate, September 19, 1940, by a vote of 44 to 30.[22]

Early in 1941, the Treasury recommended that the federal government and state and local governments be permitted to tax the interest on each other's bonds, as a complement to the abolition of the partial immunity from the federal tax of Treasury bond interest, but the suggestion was rebuffed by Congressional leaders.[23] The Treasury then attempted to have such a measure included in the revenue bill of 1941 but were advised by Ways and Means Committee leaders that it was doubtful if it would be acceptable to the Committee or the House.[24]

In 1942 the Treasury, in order to meet the need for war revenue, made a special drive to block the principal loopholes in the income tax structure, and for the first time recommended abolition of the exemption on outstanding as well as on future issues.[25] Both proposals met a barrage of opposition. The revenue bill reported by the Ways and Means Committee and passed by the House did not contain any provision concerning exemption;[26] the Senate Finance Committee's version of the bill included a provision for taxing the interest on future issues only, but after a long debate this provision was killed in the Senate on October 8, 1942, by a vote of 52 to 34.[27]

Since that time the issue has been dormant except for an occasional flareup. The writer is informed, however, that the Conference for State Defense maintains a skeleton organization against the time when the attempt to abolish exemption will be renewed.

Because of the close relations of most Congressmen with local political organizations, state and local officials can exert particularly strong pressure. The states and localities object to the abolition of their exemption on two counts; first, the increased cost of borrowing which would be imposed upon states and their subdivisions; second, the alleged danger that this would entail greater domination by the federal government over state and local finances and hence undermine the federal system. The latter objection has been the dominant theme of the opposition to abolishing exemption and has probably been stressed largely to overcome the opposition to the exemption expressed both by the public and the press following the President's special message of 1938.[28] Just how many of the bitter tears which were shed over the prospective demise of "self-government" were of the crocodile variety it is impossible to say, but Congressmen, at least, were impressed. The general tenor of the argument of the states and municipalities is indicated in the following statement by Henry Epstein, former Solicitor General of the State of New York and one of the leaders of the fight against abolition of exemption, as recently as 1945.

The tax would yield no net fiscal gain to the public as a whole . . . But that does not mean that it makes no difference whether the Federal Government may tax local borrowing or not. It makes a tremendous difference in the delicate balance of powers in our Federal System.

The last depression exploded the myth that municipal credit is indestructible. The fact is that municipal government relies on real estate taxation for about 85 per cent of its revenues. All other sources have largely been preempted by the Federal and State governments. But it is common knowledge that the real estate taxpayer is already overburdened. Raising the tax rate often increases delinquency so that you end up with even less total revenue.

Now consider the impact of a Federal tax which increases the debt service of municipal governments. And remember that debt service is frequently 25 per cent or more of the total expenditures. Either the city must curtail its functions and abandon projected capital improvements in the face of the added cost of borrowing, or it must try to raise taxes. If it curtails needed public services or declines to undertake new projects, you create a vacuum of the type which politics abhors. And the Federal Government may well move in to fill that vacuum, ready to spend the very money it has taken from the municipal treasury by taxing the city's bonds. But now the expenditure of the money is not controlled at home by the local citizen. Either it is doled back to the city from Washington, on conditions which sap the vitality and independence of local government or the Federal Government itself may undertake the abandoned local functions, again upsetting the balance between the local and central governments.

So we must conclude that the attempt to tax state and municipal financing is an attempt to end only a hypothetical evil and that it would bring down upon us the desperately real danger of disrupting the delicate balance of our federal system and the freedom of local self-government and the democracy which is the essence of self-government.[29]

CHAPTER V

_____

Effects of Eliminating Subsidies on State and Local Borrowing

THE OPPONENTS of tax exemption, before launching another all-out campaign for complete abolition, should examine more carefully the question of whether the case for eliminating the borrowing differential to the state and local governments is so compelling that it should be pressed even at the risk of sacrificing the elimination of the subsidy to upper income bondholders. This raises the following questions:

1. Would the abolition, without compensation, of the tax-exemption benefit to the states and localities be likely to have desirable effects (relative to what the situation would be if the exemption benefit were maintained) upon the volume and stability of the aggregate income flow, that is, would the probable effect be to accentuate or to dampen cyclical fluctuations?[1]

2. Would abolishing exemption be likely to promote a more progressive tax structure and a better distribution of incomes (a) among individuals? (b) among communities?

3. Would the abolition of exemption be likely to contribute markedly to improving fiscal management by eliminating uneconomic borrowing?

THE PROBLEM OF ANALYSIS

To arrive at any general conclusions on the effects of abolishing the preferential cost of borrowing to the states and localities, it would be necessary to know future magnitudes of state and local borrowing, future interest rates, future federal income tax rates, the nature of state and local tax structures in the future, the probable course of future federal-state-local relationships, and what

_____

[1] For notes to chapter v, see pages 146–150.

immediate steps would be taken by the state and local governments and by the federal government if tax exemption were
abolished. In the absence of such data, the best that can be done
is to see whether the analysis possible on the basis of the limited
information available strongly supports the case for outright
elimination of state and local borrowing advantages.[2]

The analysis is based upon the following assumptions: (1) that
federal, state, and local tax structures and relationships will not
change markedly in the period to which the analysis is applicable;
(2) that the magnitudes involved, relative to state and local
budgets and to federal budgets, will remain small, at least in the
foreseeable future. The second assumption is necessary because
the analysis concerns the effects of abolishing exemption with no
compensation to the states and localities. If the increased cost,
because of the elimination of the state and local borrowing advantage, were large, the federal government would probably be forced
to extend relief on a haphazard basis.

POSSIBLE RESPONSES TO THE ELIMINATION OF SUBSIDIZED BORROWING

If state and local exemption benefits were continued, the effect
of eliminating such benefits would be to transfer funds from the
states and localities to the federal government. The mechanism of
the "transfer" would involve incremental payments by the states
and localities to bondholders, who in turn would hand these additional receipts over to the federal government in the form of tax
payments. (It is assumed that the private subsidies to high-income
bondholders are eliminated.)

The state and local governments may adjust their budgets to
the increased interest cost (relative to what would otherwise be
the case) in at least five ways:

1. By increasing taxes.
2. By decreasing expenditures other than debt service out of taxation.
3. By decreasing new borrowing to reduce the outlay for debt service.
4. By decreasing the rate of debt retirement.
5. By decreasing cash surpluses, or reserves, which would otherwise be
built up.

Another response might be increasing short-term borrowing to meet increased current costs imposed by the additional cost of borrowing, but this would be a temporary measure only and would have to be made up eventually by adopting one or more of the five principal alternatives.

Similarly, the federal government may adjust its budget to the increased tax revenue (relative to what would otherwise be the case) in at least five ways:

1. By decreasing other tax receipts.

2. By increasing "ordinary" expenditures, for items other than debt service, out of taxation.

3. By increasing borrowing (i.e., the increased revenues might be used to service increased indebtedness).

4. By increasing cash surpluses.

5. By decreasing borrowing or increasing the rate of debt retirement by the amount of the new tax revenues.

Any analysis of combinations of such responses obviously must be greatly oversimplified. Even if the state and local governments, on the one hand, and the federal government, on the other, each could adopt only one of these alternatives at a time, there would still be twenty-five possible "simple" combinations. Actually, various governmental units might adopt any or all of these alternatives in varying proportions in "complex" combinations so that the total number of possible combinations is almost infinite.

It is possible, however, to consider the effects of any single course of action by the states and localities combined with any single course of action by the federal government. Any conclusions reached will hold even if the simple combination examined is only part of a complex combination.

At least two of the alternatives listed for the federal government seem unlikely to be adopted. The federal government has not made a practice of building up cash reserves except when financing war expenditures, nor does it seem likely to do so in the near future unless the Treasury and Congress become converted to the principles of functional finance. It seems unlikely also that the federal government would ever increase its deficit over what would otherwise be the case because of increased tax revenue, since such deficits typically are incurred because of a shortage rather than a profusion of tax revenues.

State and Local Taxes Increased

To the extent that this alternative was adopted by the states and localities, the implications for the fiscal structure would depend primarily upon what state and local taxes were increased. States and localities have relied heavily upon regressive taxes.[3]

Local governments which are responsible for approximately 85 per cent of the outstanding obligations, rely very largely on the property tax and seem likely to do so in the foreseeable future.[4] It has been pointed out that increased tax costs of local governments would not necessarily come from property taxes, since during the last few years financial pressure on localities has resulted in increased local shares of state-administered taxes and the assumption by the states of larger shares of jointly-financed functions like education and relief.[5] On the other hand, although the tendency has been for the states to move away from property taxes, the largest proportion of their increased revenues during the prewar years came from excise and general sales taxes and highway taxes. Postwar experience has followed the same pattern. In the first part of 1947, four states enacted general retail sales taxes for the first time; seven imposed new taxes on cigarettes; and a large number increased existing rates on sales of motor fuel and alcoholic beverages. Many state legislatures have recently authorized their municipalities to levy sales taxes and other taxes on consumption.[6]

In revenue-producing projects, which account for a considerable proportion of outstanding state and local debt, where the revenues are used to service the debt, increased interest charges would necessitate increased public prices relative to what otherwise would be the case. The effects of such an adjustment in many cases would be similar to those of an excise tax which reductions in federal excise taxes would no more than offset.[7]

FEDERAL TAXES REDUCED (STATE AND LOCAL TAXES
INCREASED CORRESPONDINGLY)

This alternative would have no primary effect upon aggregate income, that is, aggregate consumers' disposable income and business savings would not be changed, since increased state and local taxes would be offset by decreased federal taxes. There might be secondary effects, however, depending on the change in the distribution of income and in the over-all fiscal structure. The effect upon the progressiveness of the tax system and the distribution of income would depend upon what taxes were affected—whether the federal taxes which were reduced were more or less progressive than the state and local taxes which were increased.

Ultimately, since it is assumed that private subsidies would be eliminated, the redistribution of income resulting from this combination would be a transfer from state and local government taxpayers to federal government taxpayers. Suppose that the increased tax requirements of the state and local governments were met by property taxes, excises, and general sales taxes and increased prices for public services, while the federal government reduced income taxes. There are few *a priori* grounds for thinking that this situation would result in a more equitable fiscal structure.

What federal taxes might be reduced it is difficult to say. The federal government might undertake to eliminate its own worst taxes. These are probably excise taxes, but in peacetime federal excises have been levied principally upon items classed as luxuries or semiluxuries; such excises probably are not so socially deleterious as general sales taxes, property taxes on private homes belonging to middle- and low-income families, or even the pricing of public services above marginal cost. Granting that theoretically it would be possible to eliminate objectionable federal taxes and substitute less objectionable state and local taxes, unified action toward this end would be difficult to obtain, particularly since projects involving the abolition of the borrowing advantage of the states and localities doubtless would meet violent opposition.

Taxpayers of communities whose debt is disproportionately large, relative to wealth and federal taxes paid, probably would be affected adversely. Taxpayers in communities whose ratios of bond interest expenses to taxable income were lowest would incur relatively small additional borrowing costs and receive relatively large income or other tax reductions at the expense of taxpayers in communities with the highest ratios of bond interest to taxable income. The latter class of communities probably would include some whose absolute bonded indebtedness is low but whose interest costs, relative to taxable incomes, are relatively high because of (1) their low economic level, (2) possible mismanagement of their finances in the past, and (3) the lack of market outlets for their bonds.

The complaint is made that in order to get the exemption subsidy, states and localities must borrow. This is not the whole picture. So far as the benefit applies to refunding bonds, the requirement is only that they must have borrowed. Abolition of the exemption benefit obviously would not affect the amount of indebtedness contracted in the past, but it might increase the burden of such indebtedness.

FEDERAL EXPENDITURES INCREASED (STATE AND LOCAL TAXES INCREASED CORRESPONDINGLY)

Unless the incremental federal expenditures would be net income increasing, as they presumably would not be so far as they were financed by increased property taxes, excises and general sales taxes, low-rate income taxes, and increased prices of public services, there presumably would be little effect upon aggregate income.

Not much can be said about the effects of such an arrangement upon the fiscal system. Relative to the *status quo*, the principal effect would be that the states and localities would levy taxes which they would not levy otherwise, even if they could direct the spending of the proceeds, whereas the federal government would make expenditures which it would not make if it had to increase rates on its other tax bases. This suggests that federal expenditures financed in this way would be unlikely, at least by most *ex ante* criteria, to be highly efficient economically.[8]

The increased return from taxing state and local bond interest might be returned to the states and localities by means of a more efficient "subsidy" formula. However, since this "subsidy" would be financed, in effect, by the states and local governments out of taxes which they would not otherwise have levied, it is not likely that many of them would favor the arrangement, which would probably be regarded as federal domination. Furthermore, the greatest relative burden in some cases would probably rest upon the states and localities with the greatest need for relief from their burden of debt.

NEW FEDERAL BORROWING OR OUTSTANDING INDEBTEDNESS REDUCED (STATE AND LOCAL TAXES INCREASED CORRESPONDINGLY)

As a result of this combination, state and local taxpayers would have less purchasing power than they would have had otherwise, and potential federal bondbuyers or former bondholders would have cash instead of bonds. The immediate income effects would depend upon whether the potential federal bondbuyers would be as likely as state and local taxpayers promptly to spend the funds involved. It is probable that potential and present bondholders, deprived respectively of the opportunity to buy and hold federal bonds, would invest (or spend) the funds involved as promptly during prosperous times as would state and local taxpayers (who would possess the funds were exemption continued).[9] During depressed times they probably would be less likely to spend than state and local taxpayers. Therefore, abolition of exemption might tend to promote deflation more than it would check inflation.

In the long run, federal taxpayers would be relieved of the necessity of servicing and repaying the debt which would otherwise have been incurred or maintained, this at the expense of state and local taxpayers. The effect here would be that of a reduction in federal taxes. (Cf. the first case discussed, on pp. 62–63.)

Not much can be said about the immediate effects of the redistribution of purchasing power as between bondholders and taxpayers; probably neither will relish the situation so that the loss in satisfaction may be general. Those who oppose on principle the creation of debt may applaud, but in view of the general regressiveness of state and local tax systems, it seems at least possible that the long-term effects, which would involve relieving federal tax-payers at the expense of state and local taxpayers, might more than offset the disadvantages of incurring or maintaining additional federal debt.

State and Local Tax-Financed Expenditures (Other than for Debt Service) Reduced

Since the maintenance of debt service is likely to be one of the most inflexible items in a government's budget, and since state and local tax resources are generally limited, reducing ordinary expenditures is one of the alternatives more likely to be adopted by states and localities, particularly during depressions. The pressure to maintain debt service at the expense of social services apparently has been exacerbated during critical times in the past by the insistence of bankers upon slashing ordinary expenditures.[10]

Federal Taxes Reduced (State and Local Tax-Financed Expenditures Reduced Correspondingly)

The immediate effect in this case would be to decrease government income-creating expenditures relative to what would be the case if state and local bond interest were not taxed. Funds which the states and localities otherwise would have spent would be transferred to the beneficiaries of federal tax reductions, so that there would be a substitution of certain for potential expenditures. Since individuals benefiting from tax reductions probably would be less likely promptly to respend their increments during depressed times than during boom periods, this combination would be more likely to promote deflation than to check inflation.

From the viewpoint of the states and localities, it may be argued that state and local government functions would be impaired for the benefit of federal taxpayers. The largest relative decreases in expenditures, moreover, might be forced upon heavily indebted governments with poor credit ratings, which could least afford to decrease social service expenditures. As in the first combination, the states and localities with the largest ratios of indebtedness to income would be most heavily burdened; whereas those with the smallest ratios would receive the greatest benefit.

FEDERAL EXPENDITURES REDUCED (STATE AND
LOCAL TAX-FINANCED EXPENDITURES
DECREASED CORRESPONDINGLY)

With this combination there would be no immediate effect upon aggregate income unless the multiplier effects of marginal federal expenditures were larger or smaller, for some reason, than multiplier effects of marginal state and local expenditures.

Whether this combination would be advantageous depends upon whether marginal federal expenditures would be more socially beneficial than corresponding marginal state and local expenditures. This question is impossible to answer without knowing and analyzing in each case the marginal expenditures concerned. There is no *a priori* reason for thinking that federal expenditures would be superior; during the 1930's, for example, it was often pointed out that federal grants to alleviate unemployment often went for frills, rather than assisting states and localities to maintain necessary services.[11]

FEDERAL BORROWING OR OUTSTANDING INDEBTEDNESS
DECREASED (STATE AND LOCAL TAX-FINANCED EXPENDITURES
DECREASED CORRESPONDINGLY)

The immediate income effect in this case would depend upon whether potential federal bondholders spent or invested an amount equivalent to what they would otherwise lend to the federal government. (Cf. above, pp. 64–65.) Federal taxpayers would be relieved of interest and repayment burdens at the expense of those who otherwise would receive the benefits of the marginal state and local expenditures.

The over-all fiscal effect would be to reduce deficit-financed expenditures, since the state and local marginal expenditures, if they had been made, in effect would be financed by an increase in the federal deficit. Since decisions to decrease state and local expenditures and to reduce federal borrowing would be taken by different legislatures and administrations, such decisions would not be weighted against one another. It might be argued that state and local "ordinary" expenditures should never be financed by borrowing, especially by another government jurisdiction, but this is too easy a way of disposing of the question. The answer depends, rather, upon the nature of the expenditures which are curtailed. If the curtailment results in increased municipal efficiency so that the same services are provided at reduced cost, then the change would be all to the good. However, it seems doubtful if government efficiency would ever be greatly promoted in this manner.

STATES AND LOCALITIES REDUCE BORROWING

QUANTITATIVE EFFECT OF ABOLISHING EXEMPTION UPON STATE AND LOCAL BORROWING

The effect of exemption upon the amount of state and local borrowing has always been hotly debated, like most other aspects of this question, without producing much illumination. The elasticity of the state and local demand for loans cannot be inferred from available time series, since there seems to be no correlation between the interest rate and the amounts borrowed at various times. Much of the present debt outstanding was incurred in the 1920's, when interest rates were relatively high. (See below, Appendix A, statistics of new and refunding issues during the 1920's and 1930's, also Tables 1 and 2, average yields on high-grade municipal bonds, above, pp. 19 and 21.)

There has been little agreement about the probable effect on new municipal issues of eliminating preferential interest rates. Even the opponents of exemption have been divided on this point. It has often been charged that exemption encourages reckless and uneconomic borrowing and borrowing for "socialistic" purposes; this belief was one of the principal motivations behind the campaign waged against exemption in the early 1920's.[12]

More recently, opponents of exemption, intent on cutting off the subsidy to upper-income bondholders, have argued that the state and local demand for borrowed funds is relatively inelastic with respect to the rate of interest and that abolishing exemption would not materially impede state and local borrowing.[13] This argument is somewhat at odds, of course, with the argument that exemption is an inefficient form of subsidy because the states and localities have to borrow to take advantage of it.

On the other hand, numerous state and local fiscal authorities and investment bankers have claimed that exemption has considerably influenced the supply side of the market and that they knew of specific projects and refunding operations which could not have been initiated had bond interest been taxable, because the market would not have taken taxable bonds paying reasonable rates of interest, or, in some cases, any rates of interest. These situations seem to have been most prevalent during the depression of the 1930's.[14]

Actually, it seems probable that constitutional and statutory restrictions affect state and local borrowing considerably more than do reasonable fluctuations in the level of the rate of interest. State governments are restricted, in many cases, by constitutional provisions as to amounts which can be borrowed, the purposes to which borrowed funds can be put, interest charges, periods, and provisions of repayment, etc. Other constitutional restrictions closely hedge the taxing powers of the majority of state governments, so that they are limited as to means for servicing and repaying their obligations. Local governments face even more complex problems in that they are bound not only by state constitutional restrictions but also by statutory restrictions which they are powerless to remove.[15]

Available evidence, therefore, seems to indicate that the state and local demand for borrowed funds is generally quite inelastic with respect to the interest rate; however, it seems probable that it is less inelastic during periods of depression than during prosperous times because of (1) the strain on state and local finances arising out of shrinking tax bases and revenues and (2) the general tendency of state and local governments to retrench during hard times.

ECONOMICS OF EXEMPTION-INDUCED BORROWING

The charge that tax exemption encourages uneconomic borrowing raises the question, when is borrowing uneconomic? Is the only test that of the free market, with the price of borrowing set at competitive levels for government as well as for private borrowers? Or should social priorities be granted projects, or at least some of the projects, for which state and local governments typically bor-row—schools and hospitals, roads and bridges, municipal owner-ship of public utilities, and economic enterprises which do not attract private capital? Is all state and local borrowing uneco-nomic which is negotiated at interest rates lower than those which would prevail if state and local bonds were not tax exempt? Ob-viously not. Then is all borrowing uneconomic which would not have taken place but for exemption? This seems very doubtful.

The main problem of evaluating the economic and social merits of marginal state and local deficit-financed expenditures (i.e., those which are induced by tax exemption) concerns the amount and kind of resources which such expenditures divert from the pro-duction of other goods and services. If marginal projects employ resources which otherwise would be idle, there is no alternative cost and if the projects have any intrinsic economic and social merit they constitute a net gain to the economy at large.[16]

But the desirability of deferring projects until they can be car-ried out with a minimum alternative cost applies to state and local projects generally and not alone to those induced by tax exemp-tion. Moreover, if it is correct that the demand of muncipalities for borrowed funds is generally more inelastic during prosperity than during depression, the abolition of exemption would be expected to cut borrowing most when it was most needed to coun-ter the cycle.

If exemption-induced expenditures divert resources which other-wise would be employed by private firms, the question of alterna-tive costs enters the picture, and such expenditures must be evaluated on the basis of whether they are more beneficial eco-nomically than alternative employment of the diverted resources. This is true of any state or local expenditure, of course, but the argument against exemption-induced expenditures is that deci-sions to make them have been "distorted" by the fact that the interest cost to borrowing governments is less than private em-ployers have to pay. In a completely rational, free, and competitive market, this would be *prima facie* evidence that resources are not being used to the best advantage, that is, that they are being diverted from more useful to less useful employment. In this case, however, there is not a free market in any ordinary sense of the term, since state and local governments are impeded in their decisions to tax and to borrow by numerous constitutional and statutory restrictions. Doubtless, the leading consideration in some cases is not whether the benefits of a contemplated expenditure are greater or less than those of an equivalent private expenditure but whether, in view of the legal restrictions, the expenditure can be undertaken at all. It can be argued, therefore, that to some extent tax exemption offsets these institutional rigidities.

But it is replied that the low interest rates resulting from exemption will inevitably tempt city councils and state legislatures, which have not always been distinguished for either sturdy integrity or extraordinary financial acumen, to initiate outright "boondoggles" or at least to hesitate less about undertaking doubtful projects. Again, there are few data with which to test this presumption that rascality and poor judgment are elastic with respect to the interest rate, but, on *a priori* grounds, it seems highly questionable that raising the rate to competitive levels would improve materially the quality of fiscal discrimination. It might cut down on the number of foolish projects but it would doubtless also reduce the number of socially beneficial ones.

This again raises the question of whether tax exemption is not an inefficient device, as its opponents charge, since it probably promotes some uneconomic resource-diverting projects. Would it not be better to subsidize only the economic projects and eliminate the others?

On its face, this is a reasonable solution. But who is to determine which projects should be subsidized? Obviously, the federal government, which would grant the subsidies, is indicated. But although there are unquestionably better formulas for distributing federal funds to states and localities, there are also worse formulas. Traditionally, the federal government has thrown out patronage and pork to state and local political machines of the party in power.

Replacing the present form of tax-exemption benefit with a subsidy under the control of the federal government would give the latter greater power to integrate projects in countercyclical spending programs. However, if the state and local demand for borrowed funds is more elastic during depression than during prosperity, as seems likely, abolishing exemption would have some perverse fiscal effects.

REDUCED STATE AND LOCAL BORROWING AND POSSIBLE ALTERNATIVE RESPONSES OF THE FEDERAL GOVERNMENT

The magnitude of the effect upon federal finances would be slight relative to the effect upon state and local finances, since the revenues of the federal government would be increased only by an amount approximately equal (by hypothesis) to the interest upon the foregone state and local debt. The short-run income effects, therefore, are overweighed by the effects of reducing borrowing and are so vague as to defy analysis. The long-run effects are likewise indefinite and secondary to the foregone benefits from the deficit expenditures which otherwise would have been made. Thus any conclusions concerning the desirability of abolishing the preferential rate must be drawn from the analysis of the immediate and long-run effects of the reduction of deficit expenditures involved.

RATE OF RETIREMENT OF STATE AND LOCAL INDEBTEDNESS REDUCED

This alternative would have the short-term effect of leaving municipal bondholders in possession of obligations which otherwise would be retired. In the long run, the burden of maintaining this indebtedness and of repaying it would fall upon state and local taxpayers.

STATE AND LOCAL CASH SURPLUSES REDUCED

The possibility of states and localities countering cyclical tendencies by building up cash surpluses during periods of prosperity and high income to be used in ensuing lean years has recently received considerable attention.[17] A number of states have authorized their subdivisions to set up reserve funds for future public works.[18] This legislation has been conceived in part "as a means of avoiding the pitfalls of traditional long-term borrowing which have so often embarrassed municipalities in the past and as a phase of the trend toward pay-as-you-go financing."[19]

Whether the reduction of cash surpluses (as a result of the abolition of tax exemption on bond interest) were combined with reduced federal taxes, increased federal expenditures, or reduced federal indebtedness, the effect would be that cash which otherwise would be withdrawn from circulation during fat years (thereby decreasing inflationary pressure) would either be spent immediately by the federal government or be transferred to federal taxpayers or federal bondholders, who would be more likely to spend such funds quickly than wait for depression. The effect in any case would be to accentuate the cycle. Moreover, states and localities would be more dependent upon the federal government during lean years. Finally, by impeding pay-as-you-go financing programs, abolishing exemption would have the paradoxical effect of stimulating the creation of state and local debt.

CONCLUSION

On the basis of the available evidence, the case for the abolition of exemption to states and localities, with no compensation for the increased cost of borrowing, is not strong, either on the grounds of increased progressiveness of the tax structure, equitable treatment of different communities relative to their present debt burdens, or desirable countercyclical effects.

There are three main issues. First, is the lower cost of borrowing resulting from the exemption benefit conducive to uneconomic borrowing? So far as it relates to the uneconomic allocation of resources, exemption-induced borrowing would be uneconomic only when it diverted resources away from alternative private (or possibly federal government) uses. But unless it can be established that exemption-induced borrowing which diverts resources from private use is unjustifiable, *ipso facto*, it seems reasonable to think that abolishing exemption, by cutting off beneficial as well as foolish projects, would do harm as well as good, in what proportions it is impossible to say.

Also, borrowing may be uneconomic if it results in debt service charges which are disproportionate (however defined) to the fiscal capacity of the government unit concerned. By adding to the cost of refunding issues, however, the abolition of exemption would raise the cost of past borrowing, thus counteracting for some time the beneficial effects of any tendency to reduce new borrowing.

Second, in the long run most of the combinations of responses would relieve federal taxpayers at the expense of state and local taxpayers. Because of the high proportion of regressive taxes which characterizes state and local tax systems generally and because the limitation of new tax sources makes it seem improbable that state and local tax systems will be markedly less regressive in the near future,[20] such a result seems not likely to improve the tax structure as a whole. Improvement might be achieved if it were possible to enlist the coöperation of the states and localities generally, but this possibility seems remote for a number of reasons.

Third, the analysis indicates that in most cases there is as much reason for thinking that abolishing exemption would accentuate cyclical fluctuations as for thinking the contrary. In some cases, for example, where the effect would be to impair the accumulation of tax reserves, there would be a perverse cyclical effect.

This is not to say that the formula according to which the present "subsidy" is distributed is satisfactory by most criteria compared to other formulas, for example, formulas based upon indexes of the economic and fiscal capacities of states.[21] The fact that the present form of the "subsidy" may be relatively inefficient, however, does not mean that the fiscal system necessarily would be improved if the present "subsidy" were abolished and nothing substituted.

CHAPTER VI

Abolishing the Immunity from State Income Taxes of Federal Bond Interest

IN PROPOSALS for abolishing state and local immunity it is usually proposed to abolish the immunity of federal bond interest from state personal and corporation net income taxes.[1] Since federal immunity is open to the same objections as state and local immunity, and since there is reason to think that the federal government has never derived any benefit from this immunity,[2] any reform program should include elimination thereof.

ABOLITION OF FEDERAL IMMUNITY AS COMPENSATION TO STATES AND LOCALITIES FOR LOSS OF THEIR OWN EXEMPTION

State and local representatives have claimed in the past that abolishing the federal exemption would be inadequate compensation for the following reasons:

1. The aggregate returns to the states would be much less than the aggregate additional cost of borrowing.

2. Only states with income taxes would benefit—localities and states with no income taxes would receive no compensation.

3. Some states would not be inclined to share with their subdivisions the proceeds of taxing federal bond interest.

4. The states with accumulated wealth and large holdings of federal bonds would benefit disproportionately more than the poorer states in which the residents own relatively fewer federal bonds that could be reached for taxation.[3]

The force of the first objection has been considerably decreased by the great wartime increase in federal indebtedness. However, it is impossible to estimate, even within broad limits, whether by the

---

[1] For notes to chapter vi, see page 150.

time all tax exempts had matured and been replaced with tax-ables, the aggregate returns to state governments would be greater or less than their aggregate additional cost of borrowing. This depends upon the size of the yield differential which would other-wise maintain in the future, the amount of state and local debt outstanding, levels of state income tax rates, the number of states levying income taxes, the amount of the federal debt outstanding, and its distribution among the several states.

The following rough assumptions are probably as reasonable as any that can be made and illustrate the difficulty of drawing definite conclusions on this point.

ASSUMPTIONS OF AGGREGATE RETURNS TO STATES FROM TAXING
FEDERAL BOND INTEREST

Assumed annual interest on federal debt (billions of dollars)[a]	Assumed average rate of state tax on federal debt interest[b]	Aggregate return assuming all interest taxed (millions of dollars)	Aggregate return assuming 75 per cent of interest taxed (millions of dollars)
6	1 per cent	60	45.0
7		70	52.5
8		80	60.0
6	2 per cent	180	135.0
7		210	157.5
8		240	180.0
6	3 per cent	300	225.0
7		350	262.5
8		400	300.0

[a] The computed annual interest charge on the federal debt outstanding as of December, 1948 was $5.6 billions. Source: *Treasury Bulletin* (February, 1948), p. 17.
[b] These are highly optimistic figures. In 1947, state income tax collections (corporate and individual) were approximately 0.5 per cent of the national income.

ASSUMPTIONS OF AGGREGATE INCREASED COST TO STATES
FROM ABOLISHING EXEMPTION

Assumed size of state and local debt (billions of dollars)[a]	Additional cost of borrowing (millions of dollars), assuming an average yield differential of			
	0.5 per cent	1 per cent	1½ per cent	2 per cent
15......................	75	150	225	300
25......................	125	250	375	500
35......................	175	350	525	700

[a] Total amount of state and local debt outstanding as of June 30, 1946, estimated at $16.6 billions. Source: *Annual Report of the Secretary of the Treasury, 1947*, p. 671.

Even within the range of these estimates, aggregate returns to states and localities might be much more or much less than the aggregate additional cost of borrowing to the states and localities. However, there is no way of guessing whether actual magnitudes in (say) forty years will fall within this range of estimates.

FISCAL ASPECTS OF ABOLISHING MUTUAL EXEMPTION

There should be little or no increased cost of borrowing to the federal government, since the quantity of its bonds outstanding undoubtedly will be so great for some time to come that it will have to obtain support from all income levels if it depends upon selling to private individuals; furthermore, the federal government must pay a rate which will attract borrowers in states with no income tax. State income tax rates are so low that the quantitative effect upon the yield of federal obligations would be small in any event.

Relative to what would otherwise be the case, there would be an effect of a flow of funds from states and localities to the federal government, and a return flow, not from the federal government, but from the pockets of bondholders, particularly the rich who have been escaping state taxation on their federal bonds. For the most part, income-distribution effects, as between individuals, would be in the direction of greater equality. Private subsidies accruing to wealthy bondholders would be abolished. Interest rates on state and local obligations would rise, to the advantage of low-income and nontaxable bondholders.[4]

Proposals for the abolition of federal immunity ordinarily have specified nondiscriminatory taxation. If this specification were adopted, the states, to tax federal bond interest, would have to eliminate the exemptions which most of them grant to interest on their own indebtedness and that of their subdivisions. This might entail small increases in the total cost of state and local borrowing, which would be largely offset by the increased revenue from eliminating such exemptions.

The relative advantages to states of the abolition of the mutual immunity would depend upon the situation existing thereafter. This is impossible to predict. But assume, for purposes of illustration, that the incremental return to states from taxing federal bond interest would equal the additional cost of state and local borrowing; further, that income tax rates of all states were the same. Then states with the larger per capita holdings of federal bonds, relative to the incremental borrowing costs to themselves and their subdivisions, would be relatively better off than states with lower ratios. The latter would include some of the poorer states with high per capita burdens of indebtedness and low per capita holdings of federal bonds. Some states, with their subdivisions, would be worse off than if exemption had not been abolished.

Consequently, even if all states imposed the same income tax rates the aggregate return to the states from taxing federal bonds would have to be considerably greater than the aggregate increased cost of borrowing to the states to avoid the probability that some states, particularly some of the very poor ones, would lose by reason of the elimination of their immunity. If total revenue from taxing federal bond interest were markedly less than the increased borrowing costs, a few states might benefit on net balance, but most would probably lose.

Actually, further inequalities between different states and their subdivisions would exist because some states do not levy income taxes, some do not have progressive rate structures, and some levy lower rates than others. Abolishing federal immunity might stimulate some of the states now without income taxes to inaugurate them and might induce others to increase their rates. Although such a development would probably be viewed with equanimity by most economists, the charge would inevitably be made that this constituted coercion by the federal government and violation of states' rights.

Impact on Local Government

It is objected that the compensation resulting from the abolition of federal bond immunity would accrue only to the states and that the municipalities and other local units, which account for about 85 per cent of the total state and local debt but which do not levy income taxes (except in rare instances), would be placed at a corresponding disadvantage.

This is not an insuperable objection, however, since experience with state-collected locally-shared taxes, as well as state grants-in-aid to localities, points the way to arrangements by which the localities could be compensated by their state governments.[5]

Part Three

TECHNIQUES FOR TAXING MUNICIPAL BOND INTEREST

CHAPTER VII

Taxing Holders of Outstanding Bonds

Broadly speaking, there are two types of problems in taxing state and local bond interest. First, there are problems concerned with basic objectives and broad questions of policy, such as whether future state and local government borrowing should be "subsidized" at all and if so to what extent, and whether holders of outstanding bonds should be taxed and if so the objectives which should guide such taxation. Second, there are technical problems, concerned with methods for accomplishing the basic objectives.

Within this framework there are three subcategories of problems relating to (1) taxing "present" holders of outstanding state and local securities (i.e., owners as of the time the tax is announced); (2) taxing future buyers of outstanding securities, that is, buyers who purchase outstanding bonds from present holders; and (3) taxing buyers of future issues. The third problem is the only one that directly affects the states and localities as well as the bondholders.

The discussion thus far has led to four main conclusions: (1) the subsidy to high-income bondholders should be eliminated; (2) it is not clear that depriving states and localities of tax exemption benefits would improve the tax system, equalize income distribution, or promote economic stability; (3) the immunity of federal bond interest from state income taxation should be abolished; (4) the benefits to states and localities from abolishing federal immunity to state income taxes would bear little relation to the increased costs to individual states and their subdivisions of abolishing the immunity of municipal securities.

The principal objective indicated by these conclusions is to repair and to prevent damage to the progressive income tax structure. On that objective there can be little disagreement. The other basic objective usually advanced—eliminating the incentive to uneconomic state and local financing—cannot be accepted unreservedly so long as there is no clear evidence that eliminating the tax-exemption subsidy to state and local government, on either refunding issues or new issues, would markedly improve the fiscal structure as a whole. Consequently, even though it can be argued that there is no strong economic reason for continuing exemption "subsidies" to states and localities neither are there strong grounds for a bitter-end struggle to discontinue them, particularly if the fight, as seems likely, would be a losing one which would also cost the basic objective of abolishing private subsidies to high-income bondholders. In the first place, there is no reason to think that Congress in the near future will be any more willing to abolish state and local prerogatives in this field than it has been in the past, especially in view of the fact that the weight of conservative opinion has been added to the vociferous protests of the states and localities. Nor does it seem likely that the states and localities will moderate their stand on the issue of outright abolition of exemption, even if they are granted the right to tax federal bond interest, for the following reasons:

1. The uncertainty of future magnitudes and the possible inability of the states and localities as a whole to recover as much from taxing federal bonds as they would lose by surrendering their own immunity.

2. The possible inability of some states and their subdivisions, including the income-taxless states and some of the poorer states, to recover the additional cost of borrowing, even though the aggregate increased cost of borrowing is no greater than the additional revenue obtained from taxing federal bond interest.

3. The possible failure of states to compensate their subdivisions for increased borrowing costs incurred by the latter, and the fact that state compensation for the loss of immunity would further entangle state-local relationships.

4. The large yield differentials between tax exempts and taxables which prevailed during most of the 1940's.

For these reasons it appears that any reform program will have to accept the proposition that the principal objective is the elimination of private subsidies to high-income bondholders and that states and localities for the present must either continue to enjoy differential borrowing advantages or be compensated for the loss thereof.

The purposes of this and the following chapters are to analyze the theoretical considerations involved in designing an equitable compromise, to formulate a model tax plan which might serve as the basis of such a compromise program, and to analyze various tax plans which have been suggested in the past.

What the writer takes to be the principal objective—eliminating private subsidies to high-income bondholders—applies to holders of outstanding bonds as well as to holders of future issues. It will be argued that there is little more reason why the former, any more than the latter, should benefit from vagaries in the tax system which are largely the result of historical accident.[1]

Most of the reform drives of the past have concentrated on abolishing the exemption of future issues only. Although a number of proposals for modifying the exemption on outstanding as well as on future securities, have been advanced from time to time, most of these have been predicated mainly upon the somewhat uncritical notion that bondholders should not entirely escape taxation upon their municipal bond interest.[2] There is much difference, however, between this objective and the more fundamental one of eliminating private subsidies and particularly that quirk in the present system which allows the highest-income bondholders to collect the relatively largest subsidies. Moreover, most of the suggested compromises referred to, it develops upon analysis, would perpetuate part of the evil they were designed to correct.

SUGGESTED APPROACH

The distortion of the progressive income tax structure arising out of the exemption of outstanding bonds—that is, the subsidies to high-income bondholders at the expense of low-income bondholders and the federal government—obviously never would have obtained if tax exemption had never existed. This suggests an approach to the problem of taxing holders of outstanding bonds,

[1] For notes to chapter vii, see pages 150–153.

which is to re-create for individual bondholders and the federal government the conditions which would prevail if tax exemption had never existed. Obviously such conditions cannot be completely duplicated in practice, nor is it desirable that they should be. It is useful, however, to consider the steps which would have to be taken to duplicate them, and then to introduce modifications until a solution is reached which is administratively feasible and which does not violate existing principles of equity.

Outright Abolition of Exemption of Outstanding Bonds

Prior to 1942, there seems never to have been strong pressure for abolishing the exemption on outstanding issues. Spokesmen for the Treasury, in the drive for abolition of exemption in the late 1930's, repeatedly emphasized that the Treasury had no intention of asking for such a measure. When Secretary Morgenthau reversed this position in 1942 and demanded outright abolition of all exemption on the grounds that wartime exigencies made imperative the closing of all tax loopholes, he received little organized support with the notable exception of that coming from the C. I. O. and other left-wing groups.[3] Conservatives argued that to abolish exemption on outstanding bonds would constitute retroactive taxation and that it would be a breach of faith, since bondholders had bought their bonds with the understanding that they would be exempt; this argument weighed heavily with many Congressmen.[4] The Treasury replied (1) that no breach of faith was involved since Congress had never made commitments in the matter and since in any case no Congress has the power to bind its successors; (2) that the government is not obligated to insure private parties against losses caused by constitutional changes;[5] and (3) that purchasers of tax exempts had bought their bonds subject to the risk that exemption might be abolished and had therefore discounted this possibility in bidding for bonds in the market.

Charges and counterarguments relating to immorality and bad faith dominated the debate; there was little attempt by anyone to analyze the problem with a view of ascertaining the nature and extent of the losses which would be imposed by abolishing exemption of outstanding issues and whether compromise solutions might be worked out.

ARGUMENTS AGAINST ABOLISHING EXEMPTION ON
OUTSTANDING ISSUES

It was claimed that eliminating exemption on outstanding securities would constitute retroactive taxation and a breach of faith since bondholders, having paid for exemption in the belief that they were to be secure from the contingency of abolition, would suffer unforeseen capital losses. In itself this argument is not sufficient grounds for opposing new taxes, since any new tax usually imposes unforeseen capital losses upon someone. To have a logically consistent case, the opposition needed to show that some special capital loss was involved. Logical consistency, however, is not a prime virtue of most controversialists over tax legislation where personal interests are involved. Most of the arguments went no further than the view that abolishing exemption would destroy an income which the bondholder had bought in good faith, even if he had not paid full value for it, that is, that the bondholder is morally entitled to as much economic surplus as he can get. This may be doubted.

If there are any ethical implications in abolishing the exemption of outstanding securities they must rest upon one of two grounds: (1) that such abolition not only would confiscate economic surplus but also would absorb part of the payment without which the bondholder would not have been induced to invest, so that he suffers an "economic" deficit, (2) that abolishing exemption is confiscatory so far as it may involve the loss of all or part of the bondholder's original investment-in-exemption.

The point at which an economic surplus arises is determined by conditions peculiar to each individual bondholder; moreover, some of these considerations are entirely subjective and probably often transitory so that there is no way of estimating their weight, even by the bondholder himself. If all taxes were successfully opposed on the grounds that foreseeing them might have discouraged some investment which actually took place, the tax system might well be less onerous but much less productive. Consequently, this argument is not impressive.

ANALYSIS OF "UNDUE" CAPITAL LOSS FROM
OUTRIGHT ABOLITION

It can be argued, however, that outright abolition would involve
the loss of part of the original investment-in-exemption of some
bondholders and that this would constitute an "undue" capital
loss.

A municipal bondbuyer makes an investment-in-exemption if
there is a yield differential between the tax exempts purchased and
comparable taxable bonds, even if the price reflects a discounting
of the possibility that exemption will be abolished on future issues.
The bondholder, in return for purchasing exemption, avoids the
necessity of paying taxes upon the income which he would have
received from investing equal amounts in comparable taxables.
In effect, the investment-in-exemption is amortized by these "gross
tax savings." If the bondholder is highly supramarginal, that is, if
his average gross tax savings are relatively large, and his investment-in-exemption is relatively small, he may amortize the investment in a relatively short time. Other (marginal) bondholders may
require the full life of the bond to amortize their investment-in-
exemption; the investments of submarginal bondholders will never
be completely amortized.

Unless the bondholder has amortized all or most of his original
investment-in-exemption at the time exemption is abolished, in
most cases he will lose part of it by virtue of such abolition. There
are grounds for defining this loss as "undue," since the bondholder
is worse off than under his original alternative of purchasing taxables.[6]

Many taxable bondholders who purchased their securities before
1940 and most who purchased before 1935 have doubtless amortized their investments-in-exemption, since they sacrificed relatively little by buying tax exempts and have had a relatively long
period in which to accumulate tax savings. Bondholders who invested after 1940 and especially those who invested after 1942
paid relatively high prices for exemption and have accumulated
savings over only relatively short periods. Consequently, if exemption on outstanding bonds were abolished in the next few years,

the latter bondholders would be at a disadvantage as compared with the former; moreover, they would stand to lose part of their investments-in-exemption. In any given instance, the "undue" capital loss at the time of redemption depends upon whether the bondholder realizes a net gain or loss from his operation in tax exempts, relative to what would be the case if he had originally bought comparable taxables. If he realizes a net relative gain, then he cannot claim to have suffered an "undue" loss from the abolition of exemption. But to the extent that the loss owing to the abolition of exemption results in the bondholder's suffering a net relative loss on his operation in tax exempts, or increases the relative loss that the bondholder would have suffered anyway, it can be called an "undue" loss.[7]

GAIN OR LOSS TO BONDHOLDERS SELLING BONDS AFTER ABOLITION OF EXEMPTION AND BEFORE REDEMPTION

When bonds originally bought tax exempt are sold after the abolition of exemption, another element enters the picture—the capital gains and losses relative to what would be the case if the bondholder had originally bought taxables. It has been shown that an investor in tax-exempt bonds who sells before redemption may realize relative capital gains, which will offset the yield sacrificed, or relative capital losses, which will offset tax savings.

Abolishing exemption imposes an additional loss upon the bondholder roughly equal to (1) the decrease of gross tax savings from the time of abolition up to the time of sale plus (2) a capital loss resulting from the fact that the price obtainable for the bonds now includes no premium-for-exemption. Practically speaking, if exemption were abolished there would be no way of estimating the yield differentials which might otherwise have obtained; therefore, it is impossible to determine or even estimate the hypothetical market value of the bonds to sell tax exempt. For this reason, the loss imposed upon liquidating bondholders by abolishing exemption cannot be computed except on the basis of arbitrary assumptions of the differential which might otherwise have obtained, and the measurement of the loss is of only academic interest.

The question is whether this theoretical loss from abolishing exemption, or any part thereof, can be defined as "undue" according to present criteria. This depends, again, upon whether the bondholder realizes a net gain or loss from his operation in tax exempts, relative to what would have been the case if he had originally bought comparable taxables. To the extent that the loss owing to abolishing exemption results in the bondholder's suffering a net relative loss on his operation, or increases the relative loss that he would have suffered anyway, it is "undue."[8]

In summary, the outright abolition of exemption would discriminate against bondholders who have paid large sums for exemption, particularly in the last few years when yield differentials have been very high. Thus it would create inequities between bondholders who have paid large sums for exemption and those who have not; it would penalize submarginal bondholders while leaving many bondholders better off than if they had originally bought taxables and would deprive submarginal and nontaxable bondholders of the chance to sell their bonds at premiums and thus recoup some of the income sacrificed by having originally bought tax exempts.

POSSIBILITY OF REFUNDING "UNDUE" CAPITAL LOSSES

A possible solution to the problem might be to abolish the exemption on outstanding issues but allow present bondholders (holders as of the date of announcement of the tax) refunds of any loss of their original investments-in-exemption which are imposed thereby. Bondholders who had already amortized their investment-in-exemption would get no refunds.

This measure is open to the following objections:

(1) There is no way of determining the "undue" capital loss imposed upon present holders who sell their bonds before maturity, except on the basis of arbitrary assumptions.

(2) Calculating each bondholder's gains and losses would obviously be administratively infeasible even if the necessary arbitrary assumptions were adopted, since it would involve among other things determining the accumulated value of the gross tax saving on each single investment in every present bondholder's portfolio.

(3) To the extent that the effective tax depended upon benefits received in the past, it would be retroactive, and probably would be subject to objections on that score.

A "MODEL" TAX ON PRESENT HOLDERS

The principal object in taxing holders of outstanding securities is to restore the progressiveness of the personal income tax. At the same time, it is desirable to avoid imposing "undue" capital losses upon bondholders who have paid premiums for exemption. Finally, it is probable that any tax which would impinge upon subsidies received by high-income bondholders in the past would be deemed objectionable on the grounds that it was retroactive.

The primary aim of the following "model" tax to apply to "present" holders is to eliminate subsidies now accruing to high-income holders. It should be emphasized that this method does not involve the abolition of exemption, but merely the modification of the present system with a view of eliminating its worst abuses.

PRINCIPLE OF THE "MODEL" TAX FORMULA

The principle underlying the tax is that of recreating the situation which would exist if state and local bondholders originally had bought comparable taxable bonds. The purpose is to leave bondholders, or at least supramarginal bondholders, with the same disposable income as if they had originally purchased such comparable taxables.[9] The advantage of this approach is that it minimizes discrimination between municipal and other bondholders, between municipal bondholders who have paid heavily for exemption and those who have not, and between those who have purchased bonds of different degrees of risk and different maturities. The main disadvantage is the practical difficulty of estimating the net gain or loss currently accruing from exemption, since to do so it is necessary to estimate the yield differentials at the time of the original purchases. It is the writer's opinion, however, that yield differentials for past periods can be estimated with sufficient accuracy for practical purposes and, further, that even if the estimates are rough and doubts are resolved in favor of bondholders this plan is still superior to alternative plans that have been suggested.

Computing a bondholder's net liability under the "model" for-. mula involves essentially the following steps:

1a) Calculate what the bondholder's aggregate current income would be if the current book value of his municipals were invested at the yield obtainable on comparable taxables at the times the municipals were originally purchased.

b) Compute the income tax, at current rates, on the income determined as in (a).

2a) From the tax computed as in (1b) deduct a credit equal to the difference between the hypothetical income determined as in (1a) and the bondholder's actual current income, including income actually realized on municipal bonds.

b) The bondholder would pay this amount or the amount of the tax as calculated on his ordinary taxable income, whichever is larger.[10]

In practice, computation could be made fairly simple. The Treasury would issue a table of relative yield differentials presumed to have obtained at various times in the past; it would be simplest to express differentials as percentages of tax-exempt yields, which figures represent the percentage increases in income which presumably could have been obtained from purchasing comparable taxable bonds. To compute gross taxable income from a single investment in municipals, actual income would be increased by the percentage allowed; the amount of the increase also would be the tax credit mentioned in step 2a above.

The current income from bonds purchased at par, of course, is the bond dividend. Strictly speaking, the current income from a bond purchased at a discount is the dividend plus the amortized discount; actually, amortized discount is usually taxed as a capital gain, so that it may be advisable to compute the tax on the current dividend and to tax amortized discount as an ordinary capital gain. The current income from bonds purchased at a premium is the current dividend less amortized premium; the premium can be amortized on a straight-line or any other suitable basis.

For example, assume that a bondholder holds a 5 per cent municipal maturing in 1955, which he purchased in 1934 for $1,100.

Assume that the relative differential allowed by the Treasury is 0.30, and that the tax rate on the bondholder's marginal income is 50 per cent. The annual income from the bond is the dividend of $50 minus the amortized premium of $10 (using a straight-line basis of amortization) or $40. The hypothetical gross taxable income would be ($40 × 1.30) $52. The gross tax would be ($52 × .50) $26; the net tax is the gross tax minus the tax credit of $12, or $14. The rate in the "break-even" tax bracket would be 23 per cent; if the tax rate on the bondholder's marginal income were 23 per cent or less, he would not pay any tax under this formula.

TREATMENT OF SUBMARGINAL BONDHOLDERS

Under this arrangement, bondholders who were supramarginal in all investments would pay the entire amounts of their net subsidies, but if they were supramarginal with respect to some bonds and submarginal with respect to others they would be able to offset the subsidies on the supramarginal bonds by the loss on the submarginal bonds. Bondholders who were submarginal on net balance would not be permitted to decrease their total tax liability below the amount which they would normally pay on their ordinary taxable income by deducting their net losses from having bought tax exempts. Thus to some extent net submarginal bondholders would be discriminated against. There are other possible ways of handling the problem, some of which are mentioned below.

a) Each bondholder might be required to keep a separate record of each "single investment" in his portfolio. He would pay a tax on the supramarginal investments equal to the subsidy accruing therefrom but would not be allowed any credit on the submarginal investments. This tax would result in all holders of submarginal investments being treated alike. It is rejected, however, on grounds of undue complexity.

b) Bondholders who were submarginal on net balance might be permitted to carry over their unused credits to future years when they might be supramarginal. If they were supramarginal in any subsequent year they would be permitted to add the credit carried over to the credit calculated as in item 2a of the procedure outlined on page 90, to the extent that their tax liability was not reduced below the amount of the tax calculated on their ordinary taxable income. (Bondholders who were submarginal in one year might become supramarginal in future years because of an increase in tax rates or because of an increase in ordinary taxable incomes.)

c) Bondholders who were submarginal on net balance might be permitted to use the balance of their losses as credits against the tax liability accruing on their ordinary taxable income. In this case, item 2b of the suggested procedure (p. 90) should be stricken out. This principle might be carried still further, to the extent of granting cash refunds to bondholders whose income tax on ordinary income did not offset their current net losses on tax-exempt securities. This provision would apply to nontaxable bondholders and very low income bondholders.

The writer does not favor any of these additional provisions. It is true that the basic principle of the "model" tax is that of restoring the situation which would have prevailed in the absence of exemption, also that the general effect of exemption is that of a subsidy to supramarginal bondholders financed by levies upon submarginal bondholders. A symmetrical rearrangement would reverse this effect and provide for refunds to the latter to the extent of their net relative losses from having bought tax exempts instead of taxables. (Where the same bondholder is both supramarginal and submarginal with respect to different investments, this is to some extent provided for in the procedure outlined above.)

But the purpose of the tax, after all, is to eliminate a tax loophole which has been of principal advantage to the rich, thereby improving the progressiveness of the income tax structure and increasing the revenues of the federal government. Many submarginal bondholders would probably benefit under this plan either through increased federal expenditures or through lowered federal taxes. Second, low-income and tax-exempt bondbuyers have doubtless bought municipals for safety and diversification, which would not be much affected by this tax. Finally, low-income and nontaxable bondholders have had ample opportunity during the past few years to dispose of their tax exempts at high prices and to buy equally safe, higher yield, taxable federal bonds. Many of them have done so[11] and it is doubtful if the total number of bondholders greatly submarginal on net balance is very large.[12]

DETERMINING YIELD DIFFERENTIALS TO BE ALLOWED

Given a system under which each bondholder could compute his tax on the basis of the tax-exemption yield differentials at which his bonds originally were purchased, the advantage of the "model" tax would be that the amount of the tax on any supramarginal bondholder would be scaled to benefits actually received as measured by his marginal tax rate and the size of the tax-exemption yield differential originally purchased. In practice, we have noted, administration of the tax would require that in computing their taxes bondholders use schedules prepared by the Treasury. Preparation of such schedules would require a more extensive study of historical yield differentials than any now available, but in any case differentials would probably have to be based upon the yields of highest-grade bonds.[13] Estimates necessarily would be rough and differentials should be high enough to give bondholders the benefit of any doubt. Probably it would be preferable to use a simple schedule, even as rough as that shown in Table 5.

TABLE 5

ILLUSTRATIVE SCHEDULE OF RELATIVE YIELD DIFFERENTIALS FOR COMPUTING "MODEL" TAX

Years in which bonds were purchased	Differentials, percentages of tax-exempt yields
1919–1921	25
1922–1933	20
1934–1935	30
1936–1937	25
1938–1940	35
1941–1942	65
1943	85
1944–1946	140
1947	80
1948	50

ᵃ These figures, which are intended to be only illustrative, are adapted from Table 1, p. 19. For years in which the differentials changed rapidly it would probably be desirable to establish monthly or quarterly figures.

The yield differentials would always be subject to error, of course, particularly since it would not be practicable to differentiate between bonds of different grades and maturities and those issued by different jurisdictions, even if differentials applicable to each investment in tax-exempt bonds could be determined. Since differentials would probably be based upon the yields of high-grade bonds, the equity of the tax as between bondholders would depend upon the degree of uniformity of relative yield differentials which has maintained in the past. Presumably, there is an underlying tendency for relative yield differentials to be uniform at any given time, but market imperfections and other factors have probably resulted in considerable variations of relative yield differentials at various times.[14] Consequently, we should examine the effect upon "model" tax rates of variations in the relative yield differentials allowed for computing the tax.

For this purpose, as was pointed out above, differentials would be most conveniently expressed in the form of relatives of tax-exempt yields. As before, write Y_t for the taxable yield, Y_e for the tax-exempt yield, D for $Y_t - Y_e$, D_e for the ratio of the yield differential to the exempt yield (D/Y_e), D_t for the corresponding ratio of the yield differential to the taxable yield (D/Y_t), T_m for the rate in the "break-even" tax bracket, T_a for the effective rate of the tax on previously exempt municipal bond income, and T_t for the average tax rate applicable to an income, incremental to the bondholder's ordinary taxable income, equal to the sum of the current incomes from all his single investments in municipals increased by the yield differentials allowed by the Treasury schedule. Then for any single investment,

$$D_t = 1 - Y_e/Y_t = D_e/(1 + D_e) = T_m, \quad \text{and}$$
$$T_a = T_t - (1 - T_t)D_e.$$

The effective rate of the tax on municipal bond income is a function of T_t and D_e (D_e being the relative yield differential allowed for computing the tax). The latter two variables will not be independent in all cases; with a progressive income tax rate structure, the value of T_t may depend partly upon the values of D_e applicable to the single investments in the bondholder's portfolio, since the values of D_e determine in part the size of the hypothetical taxable income to which T_t is applicable.

We turn now to the effects upon T_a of variations of D_e, which can be taken to mean also the effect upon the tax paid by a bondholder of differences between the relative differentials allowed by the Treasury schedule and the differentials at which his bonds were purchased.

It can be shown that

$$\Delta T_a = (1 + D_e + \Delta D_e)\Delta T_t - (1 - T_t)\Delta D_e.$$

Here there may be two opposing effects. An increase (decrease) in D_e will decrease (increase) the effective rate T_a. If the variation in D_e is sufficiently large to change T_t (the change will be in the same direction), the increase (decrease) in T_t will increase (decrease) T_a.

D_e is a hyperbolic function of Y_e/Y_t and D_t; the limits of Y_e/Y_t (and D_t) are 1 and 0 (and 0 and 1), whereas the corresponding limits of D_e are 0 and ∞. The greater the effect of tax exemption upon yields, as measured by the ratio of exempt to taxable yields, the greater will be the variation of D_e corresponding to a given variation of Y_e/Y_t (or D_t). (See the comparative values of D_e and D_t, Table 1, p. 19.) Small variations in estimates, therefore, make for large variations in the value of D_e when yield differentials are large. Moreover, the larger are relative yield differentials generally, the greater are the probable variations of relative yield differentials applying to different bonds, and these variations will be magnified in the values of D_e.

The effects on the "model" tax rate of large variations of D_e, however, are modified by two factors: (1) For periods when relative differentials are high, a high differential will be allowed for computing the tax and only bondholders for whom values of T_t are large will be reached by the tax. A variation of D_e will vary the tax rate by $(1 - T_t)\Delta D_e$ (ignoring possible corresponding changes in T_t); the value of $(1 - T_t)$ obviously is small when T_t is large. (2) If the variation of D_e is large enough to change T_t, the effect of the change will partially offset the effect of the variation of D_e.

Table 6 illustrates the effect of variations of D_e upon the rate of the "model" tax on income from bonds held by individuals, at various income levels and for various combinations of municipal bond and other income.

The figures in Table 6 indicate that for periods when relative differentials generally were low, moderate variations in the size of the relative differential allowed would not greatly affect the

TABLE 6

EFFECTS ON "MODEL" TAX RATES OF VARIATIONS IN RELATIVE YIELD DIFFERENTIALS

Surtax net income			Representative values of D_e and corresponding values of D_t (per cent)[a]							
			D_e	10	15	20	30	50	100	150	200
			D_t	9	13	17	23	33	50	60	67
Ordinary taxable	Municipal bond	Total	Effective tax rates on municipal bond income corresponding to the above differentials (per cent)[b]								
	$ 5,000	$ 5,000	11	7	4	0	0	0	0	0
	10,000	10,000	16	13	10	4	0	0	0	0
$5,000	5,000	10,000	20	17	14	7	0	0	0	0
9,000	1,000	10,000	23	20	17	10	0	0	0	0
	20,000	20,000	27	24	22	17	8	0	0	0
10,000	10,000	20,000	36	33	31	26	17	0	0	0
19,000	1,000	20,000	42	39	37	31	21	0	0	0
	50,000	50,000	44	42	40	37	31	18	8	0
25,000	25,000	50,000	55	54	52	49	42	27	13	1
40,000	10,000	50,000	59	57	56	52	45	28	13	0
50,000	50,000	100,000	69	68	67	65	60	50	41	32

[a] D_t represents the rate in the "break-even" tax bracket.
[b] Computed on the basis of 1948 tax rates applying to the surtax net income of a single individual. In computing each tax rate (1) the corresponding municipal bond income was increased by the percentage of the relative differential (D_e) at the top of the column; (2) the municipal bond income plus the increase was added to ordinary income and the tax was computed for a surtax net income of this size, and (3) from the gross tax as determined in (2) was subtracted (a) the tax which would be paid on the ordinary taxable income and (b) the amount of the hypothetical increase in municipal income computed in (1). The result is the net tax on municipal bond income; dividing this by the amount of bond income gives the rate of the tax. For married couples splitting income, these rates apply to incomes twice the size of those shown.

rate of the "model" tax on the bond income of wealthy investors, where the income tax rate structure is comparable to that of 1948. On bonds acquired at high differentials—top-grade bonds acquired during the middle 1940's, for example—exemption subsidies will be small in any case. Here again doubts as to the size of the relative differential to be allowed can be resolved in favor of bondholders without seriously impairing the objective of the "model" tax, which is to tax away the bulk of exemption subsidies accruing to high-income bondholders while preserving investments-in-exemption. Another fact supporting this argument is that the periods in which relative yield differentials have been highest have coincided with the periods in which bond yields generally have been lowest.

There is some reason to think that differentials on lower-grade bonds ordinarily have been lower than those on high-grade bonds, particularly during the 1940's. If this is true, holders of lower-grade bonds would be favored by a schedule of differentials based on high-grade bond yields. This does not constitute a serious objection, however, since the proportion of lower-grade bonds has been relatively small.

COMPARISON OF "MODEL" TAX FORMULA WITH FORMULA
EMPLOYING A FIXED RELATIVE DIFFERENTIAL

A tax based on a formula which takes into account the variations of yield differentials over time is preferable, even if generous to bondholders, to one which does not. This is shown by comparing the tax based on varying differentials with a tax involving essentially the same procedure but employing a fixed relative differential. (This will be referred to as the *frd* formula.)[15]

As is shown by the figures in Table 6, a high relative differential would defeat much of the purpose of the tax by failing to reach most of the subsidies accruing on bonds purchased at low differentials. A low relative differential would confiscate investments-in-exemption on bonds bought at high differentials.

In the middle 1940's, for example, yield differentials on top-grade bonds apparently were considerably more than 100 per cent of tax-exempt yields. Suppose that under the *frd* formula the fixed differential was set at 1.00, so as not to penalize too greatly holders who acquired their bonds in that period. Under 1948 tax rates, single persons in the $20,000 income bracket (or married couples splitting incomes in the $40,000 bracket) would pay no taxes on municipal bond income, no matter at what differentials their bonds were bought. Municipal bond income of single persons in the $50,000 bracket (and married couples splitting incomes in the $100,000 bracket) would be taxed at rates ranging approximately from 17 to 30 per cent, depending upon the proportion of total income comprised by municipal bond income. As can be seen by referring to Table 6, rates based on differentials prevailing before the war would be considerably higher, so that holders of bonds acquired before the war would be favored. Using the differential suggested in Table 5 for 1935 (0.30), income from municipal bonds acquired in 1935 would be taxed to single bondholders in the $20,000 bracket at rates ranging from approximately 17 to 31 per cent, while single bondholders in the $50,000 bracket would pay from approximately 37 to 52 per cent.

In general, therefore, the *frd* formula would discriminate against bondholders who paid high prices for exemption as against those who paid low prices. Consequently, in taxing present bondholders, even rough adjustments in the schedule of relative yield differentials to the levels actually prevailing at the time of original purchases would eliminate much of the inequity inherent in the *frd* formula, particularly since the variations in relative yield differentials have been so great in the recent past.

However, if the "model" tax formula for some reason should prove unacceptable for taxing present holders, the writer would prefer the *frd* formula to most others which have been suggested.

OTHER COMMENTS ON THE "MODEL" TAX

To the extent that yield differentials can be estimated only roughly, there will be a certain amount of the same kind of discrimination in applying the "model" formula as arises in connection with the *frd* plan; but compared to other plans, the formula reduces such discrimination to a minimum. In a few cases, the formula may have the effect of confiscating part of the original investment-in-exemption. Suppose that a bondholder's position relative to a certain investment has been submarginal up until shortly before the "model" tax is inaugurated but thereafter for some reason becomes supramarginal so that he would be able completely to amortize the investment-in-exemption only if exemption were continued. The "model" tax would forestall this possibility.

The assumption that bondholders would have bought comparable taxable bonds if no tax exempts had been available is arbitrary; it is possible, for example, that some bondholders would have bought more risky higher yield securities, or that they would have engaged in profitable business ventures. This suggests the possibility of granting additional relief to bondholders who could satisfactorily demonstrate that they could have bought comparable taxable bonds yielding more than the differential allowed. Such a provision, however, would give bondholders the advantage of hindsight in concocting the most favorable deals which would have been possible at the time of their original purchases and doubtless would lead to endless disputes. Since the bondholders principally affected by this tax would be the rich and the near rich who have been receiving subsidies in the past, there need not be too much concern about minor inequities of this kind.

In summary, the "model" tax formula for taxing "present" holders would leave supramarginal bondholders as well off, after the imposition of the tax, as they would have been if they had originally bought comparable taxable securities and would leave submarginal bondholders as well off as if no tax had been imposed. In most cases, bondholders holding their bonds to redemption will be able to recover either the full value of their original investments-in-exemption or at least as much as would have been recovered if no tax had been imposed. Cases might arise where previously submarginal bondholders who become supramarginal for some reason or other would be unable to amortize their investments-in-exemption to the extent that otherwise would have been possible; however, such cases probably would be rare.

A "Model" Tax on Future Buyers of Outstanding Securities

PROBLEM OF CAPITAL LOSSES TO PRESENT HOLDERS

The principal objectives in taxing future buyers of outstanding securities are to eliminate differential subsidies to high-income buyers and to avoid imposing "undue" capital losses upon present holders who sell their bonds before redemption.

If the exemption on future buyers were completely abolished, future buyers would have no reason to prefer state and local securities over other taxable securities comparable in risk and maturity.

The yields on outstanding municipals would rise to the general level of other taxable obligations and prices would fall correspondingly. Present bondholders who were forced to sell their holdings before redemption, with no premium for tax immunity, might lose some or all of their investments-in-exemption. Such losses would be most likely to fall upon low-income or nontaxable bondholders, those who had paid the highest prices for exemption when they bought their bonds, and those who had bought their bonds most recently and would not have had time to amortize their investments-in-exemption. There is an equity argument, therefore, for measures to protect present holders against the "undue" capital losses which would be imposed by complete abolition.[16] The principal difficulty is that the "undue" loss accruing on bonds sold after the abolition of exemption but before redemption cannot be measured except on the basis of arbitrary assumptions.

If it is impossible to distinguish between "undue" capital losses and other capital losses, some sort of blanket protection must be extended to everyone. This might be done by (1) abolishing the exemption to future buyers and making refunds to liquidating bondholders, or by (2) extending a modified exemption to future bondholders which would maintain a price differential between municipal and fully taxable bonds.

The former measure, however, would involve a drastic readjustment of the whole yield structure and result in chaos in the municipal bond market, with the further likelihood of temporary maladjustments and instabilities which might inconvenience many bondholders, decrease liquidity, and endanger the success of impending new flotations. Since it seems desirable to avoid radically upsetting the municipal bond market, the second technique is indicated.

Applying the "model" tax formula for present holders to future purchasers of outstanding bonds would probably not be a satisfactory solution. Ideally, future buyers would receive full value for whatever price they paid for exemption. On the other hand, since they would get no more income net after tax from purchasing municipals than from purchasing comparable fully taxable securities, no matter what they paid for the former, most potential purchasers would probably have no inducement to buy municipals. Furthermore, the necessity of paying for something (i.e., partial exemption) the value of which would not be definitely known until after it was bought (i.e., until the Treasury had announced the allowable yield differential) probably would seem to most potential purchasers too much like buying a pig in a poke.

THE FIXED RELATIVE DIFFERENTIAL FORMULA

The object of partly exempting future buyers is to induce them to pay premiums for bonds bearing such partial exemption and at the same time avoid paying them subsidies. This can be done with the fixed relative differential formula.

The tax under this formula would be computed as follows:

1a. Calculate the bondholder's aggregate tax base by adding to ordinary taxable income (1) the current income from municipals purchased after the imposition of the tax plus (2) a "credit" equal to the current income from such municipals multiplied by the fixed relative (e.g., if the relative were 0.50 and the income from the municipals concerned were $800, the "credit" would be $400).

b) Compute the income tax, at current rates, on the base determined as in (a).

2. Deduct from the amount of the tax so computed the "credit" determined as in (1a).

The tax would tend to maintain a relationship between the market yield of any given partly tax-exempt security (Y_p) and the yield of comparable taxables (Y_t), such that $Y_p = Y_t/(1 + C_r)$, where C_r equals the fixed relative. At this value of Y_p, bondbuyers would be indifferent whether they bought municipals or fully taxable bonds. But if Y_p should rise above this point (i.e., if the price of partly exempt municipals, relative to that of comparable taxables, should fall) then investors would gain by buying the former until Y_p again fell to the point of indifference.

Suppose that fully taxable bonds comparable to a given municipal are selling to yield 4 per cent and that the relative differential is fixed at 1.00; therefore the actual market yield of the municipal should approximate 2 per cent. But suppose that the bond is actually selling for 3 per cent. Then supramarginal and (under this formula) other buyers would gain by buying the partly tax-exempt municipal until the yield fell to 2 per cent. Assume that A's marginal tax rate is 75 per cent. If he invested $1,000 in fully taxable bonds, his disposable income (net after tax) for the first year would be $10. But by buying partly tax exempts at 3 per cent, he would get a net return for the first year of $15 (i.e., his income would be $30 and his tax $15). Consequently, he would prefer to purchase the municipal until the yield fell to 2 per cent, at which point his income net after tax would be the same as on the fully taxable bonds.

SIZE OF THE FIXED RELATIVE DIFFERENTIAL TO BE ALLOWED

If C_r were based on relative yield differentials prevailing at the time of the announcement of the tax, the effect should be to maintain the price level of municipals at approximately the former level, as long as the levels of bond prices generally remained unchanged.[17]

TREATMENT OF SUBMARGINAL BONDHOLDERS[18]

Under this formula, the tax credit of submarginal holders would exceed the gross tax;[19] and they would be able to use the excess credit to reduce their tax liabilities on other income. The reason for this suggestion is that if potential buyers who would be submarginal with relation to the differential fixed were not induced to enter the market by being allowed the same disposable income (after tax) from municipals as they would receive from buying comparable fully taxable bonds, the demand for partial exemption would have to come almost entirely from marginal and supramarginal groups. But there would be a contrary tendency on the part of some present supramarginal holders to liquidate their holdings, because of the confiscation by the "model" tax of their economic surplus, if not their investments-in-exemption. Thus it is possible that the supramarginal demand might not be sufficiently great to bring the market yields into line with the statutory yield differential.[20] This arrangement would provide submarginal bondholders with the same incentive as supramarginal holders to bid municipal yields down to the point where $Y_p = Y_t/(1 + C_r)$.

To carry the principle a bit further, if it is considered desirable to attract nontaxable bondholders and bondholders with little other income, there might be included a provision for payments to such bondholders equal to the difference between the credit and the tax liability on all their income. Essentially, the cost of the modified exemption for any given schedule of tax rates is fixed by establishing the relative differential, and it makes no difference whether this cost takes the form of cash payments to nontaxable bondholders or foregone taxes on supramarginal holders.

OTHER ADVANTAGES OF THE FIXED RELATIVE
DIFFERENTIAL FORMULA

The effect of this formula would be to freeze the market value of exemption throughout the life of all outstanding bonds. Bondholders would be prevented from realizing further capital gains arising out of the increasing value of exemption.[24] But they would also be protected against possible corresponding losses. The prices of outstanding municipals, however, would still be affected by general fluctuations in bond yields, since they would be tied to the prices of comparable taxables. They would not be affected by changes in the level of income tax rates or by changes in the supply of municipals, so far as such changes were not reflected in bond yields generally.

The use of a relative, as opposed to a flat rate, differential would automatically allow for difference in yields purchased by future bondbuyers. For example, assume that the relative differential to be allowed is fixed at 1.00 and that a bondbuyer purchases a high-grade municipal bond with a short maturity to yield 0.25 per cent. He would be allowed to retain an income net after tax equal to what he would have received by keeping the same amount invested in fully taxable securities yielding 0.50 per cent. On the other hand, a bondbuyer purchasing a longer term second-grade municipal yielding 3 per cent would be allowed to retain an income net after tax equal to what he would have received if he had purchased a taxable security yielding 6 per cent.

The plan is based on the assumption that relative yield differentials applying to bonds of various types and maturities will be at least roughly uniform at the time the plan is put into effect. So far as differentials are not uniform, the plan is subject to the same objections as the "model" tax on present holders. The lower the levels of yield differentials prevailing when the plan is inaugurated, the less the variation of relative yield differentials is likely to be. But in any case, the differential should be set high enough to give bondholders the benefit of any doubt.

A TAX CREDIT OF A PERCENTAGE OF BOND INCOME

The question arises whether the "model" tax formulas would not be unduly complicated for the taxpayer. The principal problem would be one of computation, which is fairly simple. Except for a schedule of yield differentials for computing the tax, no more data are required than the taxpayer must have at present. If the "model" formulas are rejected for complexity, however, there is a still simpler device (suggested by William Vickrey,[21] and others): abolish exemption but allow municipal bondholders a tax credit of a specified percentage of municipal bond income.

If the tax credits were based on differentials prevailing when investments were made, the tax on present bondholders could be made as flexible as the "model" tax. To exempt submarginal bondholders, the percentage credit allowed on each single investment should be equal to the rate in the marginal tax bracket, as determined by the yield differentials obtaining at the time of purchase.[22] Tax credit on future purchases of outstanding bonds would be determined by the levels of differentials obtaining at the time plans for the next tax were announced. Considerations of determination of yield differentials, treatment of submarginal holders, etc., would be the same under this and the "model" plan.

This plan is probably the best alternative to the "model" tax formulas. It extracts a considerable price for simplicity, however. If the credits were determined in the manner suggested, as they should be in the interests of equitable treatment of submarginal holders, the rates on supramarginal holders usually would be considerably less than under the "model" tax.

Rates for various income levels and relative yield differentials, corresponding to the "model" tax rates shown in Table 6 (p. 96), are shown in Appendix C. It will be observed that the plan gives an advantage to bondholders in higher income brackets and to those who bought their bonds at substantial differentials.

CHAPTER VIII

Other Tax Devices for Reducing the Differential Subsidy to High-Income Bondholders

THEORETICALLY, at least, the "model" formulas discussed for taxing present and future holders of outstanding bonds seem as equitable as any that can be devised. The principal difficulty in applying the tax on present holders would be establishing past yield differentials between taxable and tax-exempt bonds. There are other modifications of this technique which would avoid the difficulty of ascertaining yield differentials but most of them are less equitable, or for other reasons are less satisfactory, than the "model" formula. Some of the principal alternative techniques are considered in the following discussion.

FLAT-RATE TAX CREDIT

This device would involve abolishing exemption on outstanding issues and allowing a fixed tax credit (as opposed to the fixed relative differential) to bondholders in compensation for the loss of their tax exemption. For example, a credit might be allowed of 0.5 per cent of the book value of municipals held, or $5 on each $1,000 of the amount currently invested. (If it is desired not to make cash refunds to nontaxable bondholders and to prevent low-income bondholders from using the credit to reduce taxes on other income, the allowable credit should not exceed the amount of the tax accruing on the previously exempt bond interest.) This plan avoids difficulties of estimating past yield differentials, but it is unsatisfactory in most other respects.

APPLICATION OF FLAT-RATE CREDIT FORMULA TO
PRESENT HOLDERS

In the first place, if applied to present holders, the formula gives an advantage to bondholders in the highest income surtax brackets and those who have paid the least for exemption. This is most easily demonstrated by comparing the formula with the formula for the "model" tax.

The "model" formula is $T_t(Y_eP) - (1 - T_t)DP$. The flat-rate credit formula is $T_e(Y_eP) - CP$, where T_e is the tax rate which would be applied to the now taxable municipal bond income and C is the tax credit, expressed as a percentage of the principal sum.

For the moment, ignore possible differences in the marginal tax rates under the two plans. Then it is clear from the respective formulas that when C exceeds $(1 - T_t)D$, the tax under the flat-rate credit plan will be smaller than the "model" tax. This will be so if C (the credit) is relatively large, if T_t is relatively large, and if D (the yield differential) is relatively small. Thus the advantages of the flat-rate credit plan, relative to the "model" plan, will accrue to the highest income bondholders (whose T_t would be relatively large), and to those who have paid the least for exemption (in which case D would be relatively small). In the event that bondholders paid no premium at the time they bought their bonds, the advantage relative to the tax under the "model" tax plan would equal the entire amount of the credit allowed under the flat-rate plan (provided it did not exceed the amount of the tax accruing on municipal bond interest). Bondholders getting little or no advantage out of the plan would include (1) those who had paid high prices for exemption because of (a) the time at which they bought their bonds or (b) the poorer quality or longer life to maturity of such bonds, and (2) those whose marginal tax rate was relatively small. However, for any bondholder the average yield differential (D) would have to be much larger than the tax credit (C), depending on the size of T_t, if the tax under the flat-rate credit plan were to be as large as that under the "model" plan.

These conclusions are not affected by dropping the assumption that T_t and T_e are approximately equal. Actually, T_t would vary materially from T_e only if D and P were relatively large. In this case, the effective rate under the flat-rate credit plan would tend to be lower because the first term in the applicable formula, $T_e(Y_eP)$ would be smaller than the first term in the "model" formula $T_t(Y_eP)$.

The flat-rate credit in effect would raise the yield of the securities affected by the amount (in per cent) of the credit while continuing tax exemption on that part of the yield represented by the credit. Thus the plan is open to the same objections as the present exemption, since it would not eliminate differential subsidies, and since the same bondholders who derive the greatest advantages from the present exemption would be best off under this plan. Finally, unless the credit were very low, it would yield considerably less revenue than the "model" tax.

The only reason for preferring this plan to the "model" tax for taxing present holders is the difficulty of establishing yield differentials upon which to base the latter. If this should prove an insuperable obstacle, the fixed relative differential plan discussed above would still be considerably superior to the flat-rate credit.

APPLICATION OF FLAT-RATE CREDIT FORMULA TO FUTURE BUYERS

This plan would not be markedly more satisfactory when applied to future buyers of either outstanding or future issues. The discrimination against bondholders who have paid high rates for exemption would not obtain, of course, since the market yield differential between municipal and fully taxable bonds would depend upon the size of the flat-rate credit extended. However, persons who bought short-term and top-quality bonds would receive the greatest advantage from the credit. This would probably tend to distort the market for municipals by putting a great premium on such securities. The greatest advantages of this plan, moreover, would accrue to the highest income bondholders.

The Glass and Magill Formulas

These plans ostensibly would continue exemption of municipal
bond interest but would tax other income at higher rates. One of
the formulas was suggested by Under Secretary of the Treasury
Roswell Magill in 1937 in an address before the National Tax
Association.[1]

... instead of treating an individual's taxable income as subject to the
lowest rates in the surtax scale and thus his tax-exempt income in effect
as excluded from taxation at the next higher rates, reverse the process.
Place his tax-exempt income at the bottom of the surtax scale and super-
impose his taxable income thereon. The tax-exempt income would not
be taxed, and the taxable income would be subjected to the higher rates
applicable in the light of the taxpayer's entire income status (p. 398).

As the writer interprets this plan, it would simply value tax
exemption at the *lowest*, rather than the *highest*, surtax rates.

The other formula was suggested by Secretary of the Treasury
Carter Glass in his annual report for 1919.

... I call attention to the urgent necessity of revision of the revenue law
so as to require that, for the purpose of ascertaining the amount of surtax payable by a taxpayer, his income from state and municipal bonds
shall be reported and included in his total income, and the portion of his
income which is subject to taxation taxed at the rates specified in the act
in respect to a total income of such amount.... It is intolerable that taxpayers should be allowed, by purchase of exempt securities, not only to
obtain exemption with respect to the income derived therefrom, but to
reduce the supertaxes upon their other income, and to have the supertaxes on their other income determined on the assumption, contrary to
fact, that they are not in possession of income derived from State and
municipal bonds.[2]

The procedure here would involve calculating the average tax
rate upon the bondholder's total income, including income from
state and local securities, and applying this average rate to taxable
income. This plan would value tax exemption at the *average* tax
rate applicable to the taxpayer's total income.

---

[1] For notes to chapter viii, see page 153.

The effect of the Magill formula is that of levying a tax calculated upon the bondholder's total income, minus a credit equal to the tax on a separate income equal to the income received from state and local bonds. The effect of the Glass plan, on the other hand, is that of levying a similar tax, minus a credit equal to the exempt income multiplied by the average rate of the tax.

The formulas for the plans are as follows:

(Magill plan) $I_w T_w - I_e T_e$
(Glass plan) $I_w T_w - I_e T_w$
I_e = income from state and local securities
I_o = other income
$I_w = (I_e + I_o)$, total income
T_e = average income tax rate on an income equal to I_e
T_w = the average income tax rate on an income equal to I_w

It is apparent from these formulas that in both plans the larger the proportion of exempt income to total income, the larger will be the credit and the less the net tax. Since T is an increasing function of I (if the tax rate is progressive), and since I_w will always be greater than I_e, except in the limiting case when they are equal, T_w will always be greater than T_e except in the limiting case. Therefore if the bondholder has other taxable income, the tax under the Magill proposal will always exceed the tax suggested by Glass.

An elaborate comparison of these taxes with the "model" tax on present holders is impossible without devising an involved formula but the following comments may be made.

In the first place, when the yield differential is zero, under the "model" formula the total tax would be equal to a straight tax on ordinary income, that is, there would be no preferential rate on municipal bond interest. In this case, therefore, the relative advantage to the bondholder under the Magill plan would be equal to the entire credit. Second, if the bondholder's entire income came from state and local securities, he would pay no tax at all under the Magill plan. Generalizing from these extreme cases, it may be said, therefore, that compared to the "model" plan, the Magill plan favors persons who receive the largest shares of their income from tax exempts and those who paid the least for the exemption privilege when they bought their securities. The advantages to such bondholders under the Glass plan would be even greater.

Thus, the taxes under these plans would bear very little relation to the differential surpluses received by state and local bondholders. Bondholders who had been getting relatively the greatest advantage from exemption would continue to do so.

Unless special provision was made for the relief of submarginal bondholders, these taxes would affect them also, leaving them worse off than they would be under the "model" plan, where they would pay no tax at all.

These proposals were advanced in order to meet the constitutional obstacles in the way of outright abolition of the exemption. But it seems questionable if either the Glass or Magill plans would have any sounder constitutional basis than the "model" tax, particularly if only outstanding bonds were affected.

One possible advantage of both these plans is that the tax would be fairly easy to compute. There is little to recommend them on other grounds; they fail to eliminate the most objectionable feature of outright tax exemption, and they would permit tax avoidance through liquidating holdings of taxable securities and increasing holdings of tax exempts. Except for submarginal bondholders (those who derive no net advantage from tax exemption per se) and for bondholders whose holdings are relatively small and who paid high prices for exemption, the yield under either of these plans would be less than that under the "model" plan. Without definite data on the ownership of tax-exempt bonds under the two types of plans, it is impossible to compare the probable aggregate revenues, but on *a priori* grounds it seems likely that the aggregate yield of the "model" tax on outstanding bonds would considerably exceed that of either the Glass or Magill measures.

Because of their manifest inequities, neither of these plans is to be recommended for taxing either present holders or future buyers. The plan involving a fixed relative differential would have many advantages over either. (See pp. 101–104.)

BRIEF COMMENTS ON OTHER PLANS

Most other plans for taxing present holders which have been suggested in the past are essentially only variations of the ones already considered. There are, for example, plans which involve the outright abolition of exemptions, with refunds in the form of cash or, possibly, federal government bonds, to compensate present bondholders for capital losses imposed thereby.[3]

The major difficulties in applying such a scheme are (1) arriving at a satisfactory definition of capital losses and (2) administration, that is, determining the refunds to which various bondholders are entitled. (See pp. 88–89.)

Other plans advocate the abolition of the exemption of future buyers of outstanding bonds only, while maintaining the full exemption of present holders; and still others would apply a modified exemption only to present holders with outright abolition of the exemption of future buyers. The objection to such plans is that they are not related to the actual gains and losses arising out of operations in tax exempts but have merely attacked the problem on a hit-or-miss basis. Some plans would extend a modified exemption only to present holders, but would compensate liquidating bondholders in some fashion for capital losses imposed by the abolition of the exemption of future holders. Again, the difficulty of defining capital losses would arise, also the objection that such measures would upset the municipal bond market.

It has also been suggested, with a view of getting around the constitutional obstacles presumably barring outright abolition of the exemption, that exemption be maintained but that municipal bondholders be subjected to a special federal estate tax which would recover an amount approximately equal to the amount lost to the federal government by reason of exemption during the life of the bondholder.[4]

The first and major problem would lie in defining the loss to the federal government. It might be defined as either (1) the sum of the amounts which the federal government would have collected if tax-exempt income received from municipal bonds in the estate had actually been taxable, or (2) the sum of the differential subsidies realized by the bondholder during the time he held the bonds. Either of these two magnitudes could be computed, at least approximately, but the computations would be laborious. The effect of either upon the bond market would be difficult to forecast, but almost certainly either plan would wipe out most of the yield differential between tax-exempt and comparable taxable bonds. This would cause capital losses to bondholders who originally bought their bonds at a differential and were forced to sell before maturity.

Serious problems would emerge with (1) bonds sold before maturity, (2) bonds transferred by gift, and (3) bonds held by corporations.

If this solution were applied to future bond issues, the states and localities would lose most of their borrowing advantages and probably would oppose the plan for that reason.

CHAPTER IX

Taxing Future Issues

THE FOLLOWING discussion is predicated upon the assumption that outright abolition of the tax exemption of future municipal bond issues, without compensation to the states and their subdivisions, will continue to be politically impossible. Granted this assumption, there are two ways of attacking the problem arising out of the exemption. The first is to abolish exemption altogether and to reimburse the states and localities for their increased cost of borrowing by direct payments from the federal government. The second way of attacking the problem is to modify the present form of the exemption so as to eliminate its worst features, while preserving a substantial part of the differential borrowing advantage to states and localities.

DIRECT REIMBURSEMENT TO STATES AND LOCALITIES

RELATION TO INCREASED COST OF BORROWING

In considering the first method, the question arises about what form federal payments should take. There are two main possibilities:

(1) Compensation might be granted specifically as a consideration for giving up tax immunity but bear no direct relation to the cost to the state and local units of surrendering their immunity.

(2) Compensation might be granted specifically in consideration for giving up tax immunity and be scaled to the added costs of borrowing imposed on each state and local unit.

The first solution raises some logical as well as political difficulties. The following questions, among others, would arise.

(a) If there were no quantitative relationship between the benefit surrendered and the compensation therefor, how could it be maintained that the latter was a *quid-pro-quo* for the former? How could states and localities be convinced that it was a *quid-pro-quo?* Would such a settlement be generally acceptable? The federal government gave considerable assistance to states and localities during the 1930's but this apparently did not moderate the opposition of the latter in the late 1930's and early 1940's to the abolition of tax immunity. In fact, that assistance was turned against the proposal for abolishing exemption, since the claim was made that the federal government had already assumed too much fiscal power and that abolishing immunity would only serve further to undermine the federal system. Such arguments appear to have little logical validity but they apparently convinced Congressmen.

(b) Upon what basis should compensation be paid? There is an argument for some form of general federal grant-in-aid to individual states which would be scaled to some index of economic and fiscal capacity such as income per capita. (See p. 149, n. 21.) It seems likely, however, that such a measure would face formidable opposition from the wealthier states and localities which have large debts.[1] Furthermore, it would be likely to arouse general opposition on the ground that it increased federal domination. Under the present system, the benefits of tax exemption are controlled automatically, if erratically, by forces operating in the market. (See chap. ii.) But the states and localities defend the system, ostensibly, at least, because of their desire to minimize possible federal intervention in state and local finances. (See pp. 56–57.)

This poses a difficult problem, since most programs to eliminate the worst abuses of the present system by substituting another form of "subsidized" borrowing would involve also substituting control by the federal government over the size and form of the "subsidy" for control by the "automatic" forces of the market. This is true no matter whether the "subsidy" takes the form of a direct grant by the federal government to states and localities or a modified or partial exemption which would involve relations only between the federal government and municipal bondholders. Some formulas have been proposed for taxing municipal bondholders which would leave the amount of the benefit to states and locali-

---

[1] For notes to chapter ix, see page 154.

ties to be determined primarily by market forces, but these solutions would only mitigate, not eliminate, the worst features of the present system.

It may be that no solution will be acceptable to the states and localities, particularly if they refuse to recognize the primary problem involved—that of the subsidy to high-income bondholders. But it seems highly unlikely that any solution will be acceptable which does not relate the compensation for the loss of immunity directly to the increased cost of borrowing imposed upon individual states and localities.

Three techniques for accomplishing this are considered in the following discussion. The first two involve arbitrary "subsidies" which would be set by the federal government at a level acceptable to the states and their subdivisions. One of these involves direct payments by the federal government to the states and localities and the other involves a modified form of tax exemption like that already recommended for taxing future buyers of outstanding issues, which would maintain a borrowing differential to states and localities while eliminating the subsidy to high-income bondholders. The third technique, which might be resorted to if the states and localities continue to insist upon a benefit established by the "automatic" forces of the market, involves outright abolition of the exemption and the distribution to the states and localities of the proceeds from taxing municipal bond interest. It is likely that a major stumbling block will be the fact that there is no way, outside of a constitutional amendment, to assure the states and localities that the "subsidy" will be continued in the future. But this is a difficulty which cannot be overcome in any case.

PROPOSAL COMBINING ABOLITION OF EXEMPTION OF FUTURE ISSUES
WITH PAYMENTS TO STATES AND LOCALITIES PROPORTIONAL
TO INTEREST COSTS ON FULLY TAXABLE ISSUES

Such a proposal was made in 1941 by Lawrence Seltzer in a paper before the National Tax Association.

. . . annual or semi-annual cash payments to state and local governments for a stipulated number of years in amounts equal to 15 per cent or thereabouts of the interest on all fully-taxable bonds that they come to have outstanding would be a good substitute for the present subsidy given by the federal government in the form of tax immunity.[2]

Seltzer did not mention taxing holders of outstanding bonds, but he did suggest that "by making the cash payments somewhat larger than the added interest costs to state and local governments of substituting fully-taxable for tax-free securities, the federal government could provide these governments with an inducement to speed their refunding operations as much as possible."[3] If the plans described above for taxing holders of outstanding issues were adopted, this suggestion would have no bearing, otherwise it might be valuable. The plan has several advantages:

1. It would eliminate completely subsidies to high-income bondholders while maintaining a differential borrowing advantage to the states and localities. As has been seen, tax formulas involving a flat-rate credit and the Glass and Magill formulas would only mitigate some of the bad features of the outright exemption without eliminating them; in fact, under the latter two plans, bondholders receiving all their income from tax exempts would be as well off as under outright exemption.

2. The plan makes the value of the exemption definite. Under the present system the value of the exemption was never definitely known in most cases and as a matter of fact seems to have been fairly small during most of the interwar period.

3. The plan is flexible with respect to securities of differing risks and maturities, since the payment is proportional to the interest charge on fully taxable bonds. In this respect, the advantage would be similar to that of the present system.[4]

The percentage of the interest cost which should be paid to the states and localities and the term over which the "subsidy" should be extended (if it is not to be a permanent fixture) depend upon how much relief it is considered desirable to extend and how little the states and localities would accept as a *quid pro quo* for relinquishing the benefits of outright exemption, assuming they would accept the plan at all. Seltzer suggested 15 per cent of interest costs[5] but the relative differentials between tax-exempt and taxable bond yields rose during the 1940's to several times that figure.

Another factor that should be taken into consideration is the benefits accruing from the abolition of the immunity of federal obligations to state personal income taxes, which should be a part of any reform program. However, fixing the percentage of cost to be paid back to the states and their subdivisions is essentially a political problem.

PLAN INVOLVING A MODIFIED TAX EXEMPTION

Essentially the same result would be achieved by a tax plan employing a fixed relative differential like that recommended for taxing future buyers of present securities; this would not involve direct transfers from the federal government to the states and localities and on that account might prove more acceptable to the latter. The formula and details of this plan have already been discussed at some length and will not be again considered here. (See pp. 101–104.)

The effect would be equivalent to allowing the borrowing governments a rebate on their cost of borrowing at competitive (taxable) rates, equal to $C_r/(1 + C_r)$ times the competitive cost (where C_r equals the fixed relative). It has the same advantages as the plan discussed immediately above in that it would completely eliminate private subsidies to individual bondholders, it is flexible, and the value of the exemption is definite.

The main advantage of the modified exemption plan, compared with the first plan, is probably the illusion that it would lend of a differential established through market forces. The main disadvantage is the complexity of the computation required of individual bondholders. Although this should not be overwhelming it is desirable, if possible, to avoid cluttering up the tax system with further complicated requirements. Also, it is possible that in some cases market forces might fail to maintain the differential between partly exempt and fully taxable yields at levels corresponding to the full value to taxpayers of the fixed relative differential, although this possibility can be minimized by provisions for keeping "submarginal" bondholders in the market. In such cases, the cost to the Treasury per dollar's compensation extended would be greater than that of making direct refunds. The plan for a tax credit is simpler and is probably the best alternative. This plan, however, retains some advantage to high-income bondholders.

This proposal has been regarded as one of last resort—to be adopted only if nothing else can surmount the barrier of state and local opposition to federal "domination." The value of the benefit to states and localities would be determined by market forces, thus removing any excuse for complaining of federal coercion. Since the subsidies otherwise now accruing to high-income bondholders would go to the states and localities, with the federal government getting nothing but the trouble of collecting and distributing the revenues, the states and localities would probably be better off than under the exemption in its present form.

The Treasury Committee rejects this compromise on the grounds that "the elaborate accounting and apportionment problems that this alleged solution would involve are so out of proportion to the revenue at stake that the proposal does not merit serious consideration."[7] But it needs demonstrating that the proposal would involve many more "accounting and apportionment problems" than the solution commended by the Committee as "simple" which involves a direct subsidy of a fixed percentage of the principal amounts of new bond issues to units which borrow in the future.[8]

Determination of the aggregate amount involved could be facilitated by including two or three additional lines upon the income tax forms used by state and local bondholders and requiring them to calculate their tax (1) by including, and (2) by not including, state and local bond interest in the tax base, and to enter the difference on a line provided for this purpose.

The revenue obtained could be distributed among the units which engage in future borrowing in proportion to fully taxable indebtedness reported as of the beginning or end of the current fiscal year. However, this formula for apportionment would give an undue advantage to issuers of short-term and high-grade securities whose interest costs would be below the average, relative to the amount of obligations outstanding, and a corresponding disadvantage to issuers of long-term and low-grade securities. Consequently, it would probably be fairer to distribute the proceeds for any given fiscal year proportionately to the interest cost incurred during that fiscal year on fully taxable issues. Neither method of distribution seems to involve many more problems than the "simple" solution suggested by the Treasury Committee.

One advantage of the first two plans discussed above compared to this plan is that the amounts of the "subsidies" under those plans would be definite and would not be affected by factors, such as fluctuating federal income tax rates, having no relation to need. However, this is an advantage to the states and localities rather than to the federal government. If they are willing to sacrifice it to preserve their "integrity" (i.e., by accepting the third plan) the federal government can scarcely object. From the viewpoint of the latter, the chief reason for preferring the first two plans is that the net cost might be less than under the third plan. But if one of the first two of these plans were adopted state and local representatives would almost certainly demand that their advantage be at least as great as that afforded by the yield differential currently prevailing. The 1945 differentials on long-term, top-grade municipals were more than 100 per cent of tax-exempt yields, and in 1948 the average differential was at least 45 per cent. (See Table 1, p. 19.) On the basis of these figures, adoption in the near future of either plan might involve a cost to the federal government of at least 30 to 50 per cent of the cost to the states and localities of borrowing at competitive taxable rates. The gain to the federal government would depend upon the amount of tax which could be collected upon municipal bond interest; this would depend in turn upon the concentration of such bonds in the hands of high-income individuals. At the present time, a high proportion of municipals is held by individuals who stand to profit from exemption. If the exemption were abolished, a larger proportion of municipals, which would then pay competitive rates of interest, probably would move into the portfolios of institutional holders, which would be nontaxable or subject only to low tax rates, so that correspondingly little revenue—perhaps less than 20 per cent of the interest involved—would be collected. Consequently, it might be cheaper to accept the third plan than to hold out for a compromise along the lines of the first two, in which the subsidies to states and localities, if fixed with reference to conditions prevailing during the past few years, would be relatively high. In any event, the third plan avoids the contentious question of the amount of the "subsidy" to be granted, whether directly or through a modified tax-exemption device. Moreover, it would probably involve less trouble to the bondholder than the fixed relative differential tax formula in the second plan. For all these reasons it deserves serious consideration.

LIMITATIONS TO MODIFIED EXEMPTION AND SUBSIDY PLANS

Essentially, the proposals suggested for continuing exemption benefits to states and localities are only stop-gap solutions and do not meet a great many urgent problems in this area.

1. They do not meet the problem that in ordinary times many small governmental units with restricted markets for their securities are forced to pay higher prices for borrowing than their credit situations would justify.[9]

2. They offer no complete solution to the problems of state and local units in times of depression, when the need for borrowing may be considerable, and when state and local credit tends to be poor because of decreased property, sales, and income tax revenues. If depressions could be eliminated this would constitute no problem, but this happy solution seems far from being assured at the present time.

3. They do not recognize the possibility that providing cheap credit will tempt politicians and administrators to financial recklessness or abuse.

4. But the most serious objection to these measures is that they are predicated, although necessarily, upon the existing fiscal system wherein governments, as in the past, go their own ways as if their own fiscal policies had no relationship with the policies of other governments. They provide no facilities for coördinating

state and local capital expenditures (in so far as would otherwise be possible) in countercyclical policy and do not even provide any incentives for leveling out such expenditures.

It has been suggested that state governments help in supervising local government loans through establishing state-local commissions such as already exist in some states,[10] where states would use various devices to support municipal credit and facilitate municipal borrowing. One such device might be the establishment of a revolving fund to which municipalities would have access. This would make it possible to cut the cost of borrowing to some communities and lessen their dependence on the open market.[11]

One of the principal advantages of such a plan would be that it would make funds available to local units at a low interest cost. Obligations held by states and by revolving funds would not be taxable, thereby preserving to some degree the advantages of tax exemption. Also, it would make possible the supervision of local borrowing and the checking of reckless expenditures. This is not a certain cure as seen by the experience with their localities of some southern states, notably Arkansas,[12] but in most cases it might bring about improvements.

Another aid, suggested by Hansen and Perloff,[13] would be for the federal government to assist state and local borrowing through the establishment of an "Intergovernmental Loan Corporation." Hansen and Perloff recommend that the Corporation "should be authorized to purchase the securities of state and local governments at a rate of interest which would reflect the cost of borrowing to the federal government plus a carrying charge (including in the computation of the charge probable losses through defaults)."[14] "The corporation should not be restricted to the financing of self-liquidating projects and should be authorized to buy the securities of any community whose economic capacity reflects the ability to pay for the loan over a long period of time."[15]

This solution would provide further assistance to states and localities, particularly the poorer ones, which are plagued by high interest costs. Such programs, if they could be established, would attack state and local financial problems on a much broader basis than that involved in the low-cost borrowing made possible by tax exemption, and would make unnecessary the continuation of the exemption, even in a modified form.

QUESTION OF CONSTITUTIONALITY

Whether the immunity established by the Pollock decisions was abolished by the sixteenth amendment has been the subject of extensive and long-continued legal controversy.[16] The Supreme Court itself has never ruled directly upon the point. Nevertheless, in the past few years a long list of decisions has steadily narrowed the once-sweeping immunity of state and local agencies and instrumentalities.[17]

In the 1920's and early 1930's it was generally conceded that abolishing municipal bond interest immunity could be accomplished only by a constitutional amendment. Recently, however, the weight of opinion of students of constitutional law has inclined toward the view that the present Court would uphold legislation to tax state and local bond interest, particularly in view of the Court's liberal attitude on Congressional authority. State and local representatives, however, profess to see ample reason for thinking that the Pollock decision is still good law.[18]

The most recent Supreme Court decision on federal taxation of state instrumentalities was handed down in the Saratoga Springs case,[19] in which the Court upheld the right of the federal government to levy a tax on the sale of bottled mineral waters by the State of New York. In the decision the Court set out to reëxamine the entire question of state and local immunity; however, the various opinions shed little light on what the Court would do about taxing bond interest. At least three different views relating to state immunity were expressed. On one hand, Justice Frankfurter, joined by Justice Rutledge, seemed to indicate that where discrimination is absent questions of immunity are no longer a subject for judicial review.[20] Four justices[21] kept to the middle of a well-trodden road, maintaining that the test should be whether "the tax unduly interferes with the performance of the States' functions of government. If it does, then the fact that the tax is non-discriminatory does not save it."[22]

Justices Douglas and Black, on the other hand, sharply condemned the trend toward narrowing state and local immunity and rejected the distinction, established in the case of South Carolina v. U.S.[23] between activities of a state which are and those which are not strictly governmental.[24] Consequently, there is some question whether the Court would uphold legislation for outright abolition of the exemption of future issues. On the other hand, if legislation for a compromise solution, such as one of the three discussed above, were adopted, it might be harder to demonstrate to the Court that the "states' functions of government" were "unduly" interfered with, especially in view of the Court's recent disinclination to nullify acts of Congress.

No matter what the probable attitude of the Court, the state and local representatives may be expected to press for a constitutional amendment in connection with any compromise solution in order to insure the perpetuation of any arrangement which is made. The introduction of such a rigidity, however, seems highly undesirable in view of the rapid changes which may be expected to occur in state and local fiscal relations in the next few decades. Furthermore, the amending process, even if successful, would doubtless take years to consummate.

CHAPTER X

Summary

Two main conclusions indicated by this study are (1) that the private "subsidies" to high-income bondholders arising out of the present form of tax exemption should be abolished; and (2) that there is not a clear case for abolishing the borrowing "subsidy" to the states and localities. The most that can be said is that the present form of the latter "subsidy" is inefficient, economically speaking, compared with other possible formulas. The states and localities defend their present borrowing differential on the grounds that it is established by the forces of the market, rather than by the federal government, and thus assures them against possible coercion by the latter. State and local officials may be expected to oppose the abolition of their borrowing advantage as hotly in the future as in the past, and it has been demonstrated on several occasions that they can block remedial action. There is also some question as to the constitutionality of legislation which would abolish the exemption outright.

These considerations indicate a need for a solution which will eliminate private subsidies to high-income bondholders while maintaining a differential borrowing advantage to the states and their subdivisions.

There are three main problems of taxation, concerning (1) present holders of outstanding bonds, (2) future buyers of outstanding bonds, and (3) buyers of future new and refunding issues. The writer advocates taxing all of these categories of bondholders as part of a general plan.

There is an argument against outright abolition of the exemption to present holders of outstanding bonds—on the ground that this would confiscate part of their original "investments-in-exemption"—but not for letting them go entirely free. The first part of the plan is a "model" tax upon present holders, the purpose of which is to leave them with the same amount of income, net after tax, as they would have had if they had originally bought comparable taxable issues.

The second part is a "model" tax upon future buyers of outstanding bonds; the principal purpose of this tax is to eliminate the differential subsidies to high-income bondholders while (a) avoiding "undue" capital losses to present holders who sell their bonds before redemption and (b) preventing present holders from realizing large "unearned increments" from the possible appreciation of the value of exemption such as might accrue if exemption were maintained on present but abolished on future issues.

Although the tax formulas proposed are both parts of a general plan which also involves taxing future issues, no part is essential to the others. The strongest political opposition is likely to arise in connection with the plan for taxing differential subsidies away from supramarginal present holders. There seems to be no good reason why such subsidies should not be taxed, particularly if bondholders are given the opportunity of liquidating their holdings without incurring "undue" capital losses. But should the opposition prove sufficiently strong to defeat this part of the plan, it would still be desirable to tax future buyers of outstanding bonds, since the main objections likely to be raised in connection with the proposal for taxing present holders of outstanding bonds do not apply to taxing future buyers thereof. The states and localities have no immediate interest in either question, since their interest costs are not affected.

What can be done about taxing the interest on future new and refunding issues probably depends to a large extent upon what state and local officials, whose collective voice is heard through the medium of their various organizations, will accept. From the inferences which can be drawn from the available evidence, it is not clear that outright abolition of the borrowing "subsidy" would markedly improve the tax and fiscal system. There is no doubt but that compared to some other subsidies the exemption subsidy in its present form is, as its opponents have charged, erratic and inefficient. But this is an argument for improving its present form and not for abolishing it outright. Considered only from the economic point of view, it would be more efficient to distribute equal amounts through some other formula; this, however, ignores the point of view of the representatives of the states and localities, who do not regard the interest cost differential as a subsidy and who have repeatedly expressed their opposition to any substitute form of subsidy which would be under the control of and allocated by the federal government. Considering the impressive political strength of organized state and local representatives, there seems little likelihood that they will accede to such a substitution or that it can be put through over their determined opposition.

This indicates that compensation to the states and localities for surrendering the advantage of the present immunity of their bonds at least will have to be scaled to the increased cost of borrowing. To accomplish this, three alternative plans are suggested. The first two plans would offer the states and localities a definite percentage of their interest costs as compensation for the loss of their immunity "rights"—one involves direct relations between the states and localities and the federal government, and the other would work through the mechanism of the bond market. Under either arrangement the amount of the "subsidy" would be definite and not dependent upon the level of the federal income tax or erratic market factors.

The chief obstacle to either arrangement is likely to be the objection by the states and localities that the federal government still controls the amount of the subsidy. Furthermore, if an arrangement of this sort were put into practice in the near future and the subsidy were based upon recent experience, the federal government might have to assume for an indefinite period the commitment of paying from one-third to one-half the cost of state and local borrowing at competitive rates. Thus the cost to the federal government might easily exceed the revenue gained.

The third proposal is that the exemption on future states and local issues be eliminated and that the federal government distribute to states and localities the amounts collected from taxing the interest on such issues. Such a plan would preclude the federal government's incurring a loss from taxing municipal bond interest, a contingency not inconceivable if either of the first two plans mentioned were adopted.

Regardless of the probable attitude of the Supreme Court on any of these alternative solutions, state and local representatives will in any case probably press for a constitutional amendment to cover any compromise plan. But the amending process would be time consuming and, in addition, would introduce an undesirable rigidity into the system.

All of these compromises on future issues are unsatisfactory in that they do not recognize many of the basic problems involved and are predicated upon traditional concepts of financial anarchy at the state and local level. It would be much better to attack the problem through a program of rationalizing federal, state and local fiscal relations; some suggestions along this line have been offered. For the present, however, political exigencies seem to indicate an approach along more practical lines if the ancient evil is to be eliminated.

APPENDIXES

Appendixes

Gross and Net Increase in Permanent Municipal Indebtedness
(Millions of dollars)

Year	New bond issues	Old issues retired	New additions to debt
1924	1,399	262	1,137
1925	1,400	284	1,115
1926	1,365	338	1,028
1927	1,510	387	1,123
1928	1,415	456	959
1929	1,431	454	977
1930	1,487	488	999
1931	1,256	506	750
1932	849	526	323
1933	520	546	−26
1934	939	630	309
1935	1,220	871	349
1936	1,117	786	331
1937	902	794	108
1938	1,110	827	273
1939	1,126	894	232
1940	1,234	968	266
1941	1,229	711	518
1942	576	833	−257
1943	508	1,028	−520
1944	712	1,448	−736
1945	819	1,398	−579
1946	1,204	1,664	−460
1947	2,354	1,610	744

Source: 1924–1940 inclusive, *State and Municipal Compendium*, Pt. I, June 30, 1942, p. 4. 1941–1947 inclusive, derived from estimates furnished by the *Bond Buyer*.

APPENDIX B

AVERAGES OF MUNICIPAL AND CORPORATE BOND YIELDS

Compiled by Professor Lucile Derrick

Year	Corporate[a] yields	Municipal[a] yields	Difference[b]	Difference as[b] percentage of municipal yields
1919	5.34	4.20	1.14	27
1920	5.92	4.54	1.38	30
1921	5.82	4.70	1.12	24
1922	5.08	4.09	.99	24
1923	5.07	4.05	1.02	25
1924	5.00	4.00	1.00	25
1925	4.84	3.97	0.87	22
1926	4.72	3.98	0.75	19
1927	4.55	3.91	0.64	16
1928	4.50	3.92	0.58	15
1929	4.79	4.20	0.59	14
1930	4.63	3.97	0.66	17
1931	4.50	3.72	0.78	21
1932	5.26	3.96	1.30	33
1933	4.65	3.69	0.96	26
1934	4.06	3.20	0.86	27
1935	3.50	2.73	0.77	28
1936	3.22	2.57	0.65	25
1937	3.27	2.62	0.65	25
1938	3.21	2.29	0.92	40
1939	2.96	2.06	0.90	44
1940	2.88	1.90	0.98	52
1941	2.82	1.61	1.21	75

[a] *Journal of Business*, University of Chicago, October, 1946, Pt. 2, p. 40.
[b] Computed by the author.

APPENDIX C

THE PERCENTAGE OF INCOME CREDIT PLAN

The effective tax rate on the income from any single investment in municipals is the regular income tax rate applicable to the income, minus a credit. It is suggested in the text (p. 104) that the percentage credit allowed present bondholders should be equal to the rate in the marginal tax bracket, as determined by the levels of yield differentials obtaining at the time a single investment was made. The credit allowed future purchasers of outstanding bonds would be determined by the differentials obtaining at the time plans for the new tax were announced. The plan might also be used in connection with future issues of municipal bonds, as a means of continuing the borrowing advantage of states and localities.

The tax rate equals $T_e - T_m$, writing T_e for the regular income tax rate applicable to an income equal to the bondholder's municipal bond income, and T_m for the rate in the marginal tax bracket ($= D_t = D_e/(1 + D_e)$). The "model" tax rate is $T_t - (1 - T_t)D_e$. It can be shown that the rate under the alternative plan is less than the "model" tax rate by $(T_t - T_e) + (T_t - T_m)D_e$. (For notation, see pp. 94–95.)

Refer to the example on pages 91–92. The income tax rate applicable to the bondholder's marginal income is 0.50, and the rate in the marginal or "break-even" tax bracket is 0.23. Under the percentage of income credit plan, the effective rate of the tax is (0.50−0.23)0.27. Under the model formula, the effective rate of the tax is 0.35. (Here T_e and T_t are assumed to be equal.)

The rates under this plan, based upon 1948 income tax rates, corresponding to various income levels and relative yield differentials are shown in the following table. They may be compared with corresponding rates under the "model" tax, shown in Table 6, p. 96.

EFFECTIVE TAX RATES UNDER THE PERCENTAGE OF INCOME CREDIT PLAN

Surtax net income			Representative Values of D_e and Corresponding Values of D_t[a]								
Ordinary taxable	Municipal bond	Total	D_e 10 D_t 9	15 13	20 17	30 23	50 33	100 50	150 60	200 67	
			Effective tax rates on municipal bond income corresponding to the above differentials (per cent)[b]								
5,000	$ 5,000	$ 5,000	10	6	2	0	0	0	0	0	
	10,000	10,000	14	10	6	0	0	0	0	0	
5,000	5,000	10,000	18	14	10	4	0	0	0	0	
9,000	1,000	10,000	21	17	13	7	0	0	0	0	
	20,000	20,000	23	19	15	9	0	0	0	0	
10,000	10,000	20,000	32	28	24	18	7	0	0	0	
19,000	1,000	20,000	38	34	30	24	13	0	0	0	
	50,000	50,000	38	34	30	24	14	0	0	0	
25,000	25,000	50,000	50	46	42	36	25	8	0	0	
40,000	10,000	50,000	53	49	46	39	29	12	2	0	
50,000	50,000	100,000	62	58	55	48	38	21	11	5	

[a] D_t represents the rate in the "break-even" tax bracket, and the percentage of bond income that would be allowed as a tax credit.

[b] Computed on the basis of 1948 tax rates applying to the surtax net income of a single individual. In computing each tax rate (1) the income tax rate applying to the municipal bond income was found; (2) from this was subtracted the rate in the marginal or "break-even" tax bracket corresponding to each value of the relative differentials (D_e and D_t).

NOTES

Notes

NOTES TO CHAPTER I

[1] *Congressional Record*, 53d Cong., 2 sess., (1894), pp. 6804 ff.

[2] Pollock *v.* Farmers' Loan and Trust Company, 157 U. S. 429 (1895), and 158 U. S. 601 (1895).

[3] See Alden L. Powell, *National Taxation of State Instrumentalities*, Illinois Studies in the Social Sciences, Vol. XX, No. 4 (Urbana: University of Illinois Press, 1936), chap. iv.

[4] *Proposed Amendments to the Constitution of the United States Introduced in Congress from December 6, 1926 to January 3, 1941*, compiled under the direction of Edwin A. Halsey, Secretary of the U. S. Senate, U. S. Government Printing Office, 1941. The other two subjects most frequently dealt with were repeal or modification of the eighteenth amendment: 49 proposed amendments; and the method of amending the Constitution: 39 proposed amendments.

[5] Beardsley Ruml and H. Chr. Sonne, *Fiscal and Monetary Policy*, a memorandum prepared at the request of the Business Committee of the National Planning Association (Washington: 1944); and *A Postwar Federal Tax Plan for High Employment*, proposed by the Research Committee of the Committee for Economic Development (New York: 1944).

NOTES TO CHAPTER II

[1] In accordance with prevailing usage the term "municipal" is used to designate both state and local bonds.

[2] The yield differential on a given tax-exempt bond sold at a given time may also be thought of as the difference between the yield at which it is currently marketed and the yield which it would command if the abolition of tax exemption had been announced shortly before. These two ways of looking at the yield differential are not quite the same, since abolishing exemption would have a tendency to raise the yields of previously exempt securities and to lower the yields of previously fully taxable securities. However, the supply of tax-exempt securities has been so small, compared to outstanding taxable securities, that abolishing exemption at any time would probably have had only a slight effect on the prices of the latter as a whole. The ratio of net state and local debt to total net debt outstanding at various times in the past is shown by the following figures:

Year	Percentage, net state and local to total net debt
1920	4.4
1925	6.1
1930	7.3
1935	9.7
1940	8.6
1946	3.5

SOURCE: *Survey of Current Business*, September, 1947, p. 14.

[3] Or, alternatively, the tax-exempt yield will be established at the point where the total demand for tax-exempt bonds equals the total supply, both old and new.

It is assumed in this discussion that the entire return on taxable bonds is taxed like other income, also that the entire return on tax-exempt bonds is tax exempt. Under present tax practices, both of these assumptions must be modified in some cases. See the discussion, pp. 31–36.

[4] Marginal bondbuyers by this definition are those for whom income net after tax would be the same whether they purchased tax exempts or comparable taxables. In another sense, however, marginal bondbuyers are those for whom the value of exemption is just large enough to induce them to purchase tax exempts. With bondbuyers who are influenced solely by yields obtainable, the margin will be the same under both definitions. See p. 42, for a further discussion of this point.

[5] On June 30, 1941, privately held tax-exempt municipal securities outstanding totaled $15.4 billion, of which $7.8 billion, or 51 per cent, was estimated to be held by private individuals. On June 30, 1946, the corresponding total was $12.8 billion, of which $6.8 billion, or 53 per cent, was estimated to be held by private individuals. (*Annual Report of the Secretary of the Treasury*, 1946, pp. 671–672. "Private individuals" includes unincorporated business, partnerships, and personal trust accounts.)

[6] See, for example, Harry G. Guthmann's testimony before the Tax Court in the case of Commissioner *v.* Estate of Alexander Shamberg, Docket No. 107713 (1943), Tax Court of the United States. The record of the testimony examined by the writer is an Appendix to Brief for Respondent on Review, U. S. Circuit Court of Appeals for the Second District, pp. 877–879.

[7] Lucile Derrick, "Exemption of Security Interest from Income Taxes in the United States" (Studies in Business Administration, Vol. XVI, No. 4), *The Journal of Business of the University of Chicago* (October, 1946), pt. 2.

[8] In measuring yield differentials between the tax-exempt and taxable bonds, Professor Derrick used average annual yields of forty-one high-grade corporate bonds and forty-one municipal bonds, matched as to quality rating, coupon rate, and maturity. For purposes of the multiple correlation analysis, corporate bond yields were expressed as relatives of the municipal yields. *Ibid.,* pp. 38–41.

[9] In constructing this average, the surtax rates above the marginal rate were weighted by the amounts of taxes paid by the income groups falling in the corresponding surtax bracket. *Ibid.,* p. 41.

[10] *Ibid.,* pp. 44–46.

[11] *Ibid.*

[12] *Ibid.*

[13] See Frederick R. Macaulay, *The Movements of Interest Rates, Bond Yields and Stock Prices in the United States since 1856* (New York: National Bureau of Economic Research, 1938), pp. 24–29; also W. Braddock Hickman, "The Term Structure of Interest Rates, An Exploratory Analysis" (National Bureau of Economic Research, MS. November, 1942), chap. v.

[14] David Durand and Willis J. Winn, *Basic Yields of Bonds, 1926–1947: Their Measurement and Pattern*, Technical Paper 6, National Bureau of Economic Research (New York: 1947), pp. 31–40. The reasons for this phenomenon are not entirely clear. One common explanation is that many investors simply dislike paying high premiums for bonds, perhaps because of a feeling that bonds selling considerably over par are overpriced, or perhaps because of their accounting practices. Some investors do not amortize or make

any charges for premiums paid for securities, and some merely write off premiums as a charge against capital or surplus. Under the latter practice, a substantial premium would involve a substantial charge against capital. There has been a strong demand on the part of dealers for bonds nearing maturity and selling at premiums, however, since dealers for the purposes of taxation may treat such bonds as inventory and offset the loss represented by the amortized premium against other income.

[15] The Public Debt Act of 1941 provided for full taxation under the federal income tax of interest on federal obligations issued after February 28, 1941, but interest from federal obligations is still exempt from state and local income taxes.

[16] See Macaulay, *op. cit.*, chaps. iii–iv; Durand and Winn, *op. cit.*; and Durand, *Basic Yields of Corporate Bonds 1900–1942*, Technical Paper 3, National Bureau of Economic Research (New York: 1942).

[17] Durand and Winn, *op. cit.*

[18] Source: Moody's Bond Yield Averages (mimeographed), prepared by Moody's Investors' Service. For earlier periods compare the indexes of high-grade bond yields compiled by the Standard Statistics Company, *Standard Trade and Securities, Basic Statistics* (New York: 1936).

[19] Derrick, *op. cit.*, appendix. Her list of bonds includes 29 rails, 10 utilities, and 2 industrials.

[20] Cf. Derrick's averages, appendix B.

[21] These series are all unweighted arithmetic averages of yields as computed from retail bond prices or quotations. Professor Derrick's municipal series usually includes forty-one bonds; individual bonds were dropped from the series, however, in years when their ratings fell below Aaa and after their terms to maturity decreased to less than ten years. The yields are computed from bid quotations, which ordinarily would give higher yields than would ask quotations or an average of bid and ask. The Moody series of Aaa municipal yields has usually included four or five bonds of an average term to maturity of about twenty years; the yields are based primarily on ask quotations. The subgroups of the Moody corporate series (rails, utilities and industrials) have included from five to ten bonds; the yields since 1931 are based on daily closing quotations. The average term to maturity of the bonds has usually exceeded twenty years.

[22] Source: *Treasury Bulletin.*

[23] Durand and Winn, *op. cit.*, p. 14.

[24] *Standard Trade and Securities, op. cit.*

[25] Write Y_t for the taxable yield, Y_e for the tax-exempt yield, D ($= Y_t - Y_e$) for the absolute differential, D_e and D_t for the ratios of the absolute differential to the tax-exempt and taxable yields, respectively, and T_m for the tax rate in the "break-even" tax bracket. Then

$$D_t = 1 - Y_e / Y_t = D_e / (1 + D_e) = T_m .$$

Bondholders are supramarginal if the tax rate on their marginal income exceeds D_t and submarginal in the contrary case.

[26] *Annual Report of the Secretary of the Treasury for 1947*, p. 519.

[27] Although the amount of tax-exempt municipals held by the public decreased from $15.4 to $12.8 billion between June 30, 1941 and June 30, 1946, holdings of commercial banks increased from $3.7 to $4.1 billion, or from 23 to 32 per cent of the total publicly held debt. In the same period, holdings of individuals fell from $7.9 to $6.8 billion, but the percentage increased from 51 to 53 per cent of the total. Insurance companies, mutual

savings banks, and other corporations and associations, most of which did not benefit so much from tax exemption, liquidated the bulk of their holdings during this period. The excess profits tax was repealed as of January 1, 1946, but commercial banks continued to acquire municipals; in the fiscal year ending June 30, 1947, publicly held debt increased by $0.8 billion, and commercial bank holdings increased by $0.9 billion; most of the increase in commercial bank holdings was probably in short-term obligations. During this period, however, relative yield differentials apparently declined sharply. *Ibid.*

[28] Durand and Winn, *op. cit.*, p. 14.

[29] *Ibid.*, pp. 1-10.

[30] See, for example, J. R. Hicks, *Value and Capital* (Oxford: 1939), chap. xi. A detailed analysis of the theoretical and institutional forces which may be expected to affect the term structure of interest rates is given by Hickman, *The Term Structure of Interest Rates, op. cit.*

[31] Something like this seems to have happened before the war. A memorandum on yield differentials prepared by the Treasury for the Special Senate Committee investigating tax-exempt securities and salaries in 1939 reads in part, "The situation with respect to short-term securities tends to be quite different from long term due to the overpowering demand for them on the part of institutional investors to whom tax exemption is a minor consideration." *Taxation of Governmental Securities and Salaries, Hearings before the Special Committee on Taxation of Governmental Securities and Salaries*, U. S. Senate, 76th Cong., 1 sess., 1939, pp. 644-646.

[32] Macaulay, *op. cit.*, chap. iii.

[33] A census by the Moody organization in 1939 showed that of all municipals rated by Moody's (approximately 94 per cent of the total), approximately 73 per cent were rated Aaa, Aa, and A. (Reported in a letter to Harry Guthman, Shamberg case, *op. cit.*, Respondent's Exhibit HHH.) In 1948, this percentage was approximately 85 per cent. (Reported in a letter to the writer.)

NOTES TO CHAPTER III

[1] Assume, for the moment, that the return on taxable bonds (as opposed to current interest payments, hereafter referred to as "dividends") is taxed like ordinary income and that the return from municipals is entirely tax exempt. (These assumptions are later modified.)

Let P = the book value, as of the beginning of the tax period, of a given "single investment" in tax-exempt bonds. "Single investment" refers to bonds of a given issue acquired in a single transaction.

In accordance with customary usages of accrual accounting, the "book value" is defined as the original purchase price of the investment, plus the amortized discount or minus the amortized premium. The income from a given bond is usually measured over the dividend period and is found by multiplying the book value of the bond at the beginning of the dividend period by the yield originally purchased; this in turn equals the bond dividend plus the amortized discount or minus the amortized premium, for the period.

For convenience, it is assumed in the following discussion that dividend periods and tax periods are synonymous and that dividends are paid and interest is compounded annually.

Y_e = the tax-exempt yield originally purchased.

Y_t = the yield obtainable on comparable taxable bonds at the time of the original purchase.

$D = (Y_t - Y_e) =$ the differential between the tax-exempt and taxable yields.

$T_t =$ the average tax rate which would currently apply to a hypothetical income, incremental to the bondholder's other taxable income, equal to the book values of all the bondholder's single investments in tax exempts multiplied by the respective taxable yields originally obtainable; that is, the average tax rate which would currently apply to an incremental income equal to the sum of the values of $Y_t P$ for all the single tax-exempt investments in the bondholder's portfolio.

$R =$ the redemption price of the bonds comprising the single investment. For convenience it is assumed that R is par.

$C =$ the contractual rate of interest, here referred to as the "coupon" rate.

$n =$ the number of years to the redemption of the bonds comprising the single investment.

With serial bonds, the bonds of a given maturity would be treated as single investments. With callable bonds bought at a premium the practice is to calculate the yield by amortizing the premium to the earliest call date, and n would represent the number of years to the earliest call date. In practice, this question would seldom arise, since most state and local bonds have been issued without the call feature.

The premium for exemption for a single investment in bonds purchased at par equals

1. $(PD)a_{\overline{n}|r}$

where PD equals the income sacrificed annually and $a_{\overline{n}|r}$ equals $\dfrac{1 - (1+r)^{-n}}{r}$, the present

value of an annuity of 1 for n years.

The discount rate, r, equals Y_t, the yield obtainable on comparable taxable bonds. The reason is that a potential bondbuyer weighing the advantages of an alternative investment in taxable bonds would discount the income sacrificed by buying tax exempts at the taxable rather than the tax-exempt yield, since he would reason that he could invest at the higher return. [With taxable bonds bought at a discount, part of the effective return (i.e., the yield) is in effect reinvested at the taxable yield as the discount is amortized.]

[2] Since the bond by assumption sells at par to yield Y_e, it would have to sell at a discount to yield Y_t. The price of a bond to yield a certain rate r (in this case, Y_t) equals the present value of the redemption price plus the sum of the present values of the dividends it will pay, or

$$P = R(1+r)^{-n} + (RC)a_{\overline{n}|r}, \qquad \text{which equals} \qquad R - R(r - C)a_{\overline{n}|r}.$$

In the second version, the price equals the redemption value minus a discount or plus a premium equalling $R(r - C)a_{\overline{n}|r}$. In the present case, $R = P$, $C = Y_e$, $r = Y_t$. Consequently, the difference between the price of the bond to sell tax exempt at par $(= R)$ and its price to sell taxable equals $P(Y_t - Y_e)a_{\overline{n}|r}$, which equals $(PD)a_{\overline{n}|r}$.

[3] Tables prepared by bond houses showing the advantage to bondholders in various income surtax brackets of buying tax exempts are usually constructed on the assumption that alternative taxable investments would be bought at par.

The use of this convention raises some difficulties concerning tax exempts bought at markedly high premiums which, as has been seen, ordinarily sell to yield more than bonds identical in risk and maturity but bearing lower coupons. With such bonds, part of the value of tax exemption would be obscured by the use of this convention, since the differential would tend to be smaller for higher than for lower coupon bonds. (See p. 13.) There is no satisfactory way of avoiding this difficulty, however, save possibly by some arbitrary adjustment of the yield of high-coupon bonds to make them comparable to the yield of bonds similar save as to coupon which are selling near par.

[4] Assuming that dividends are paid and interest is compounded annually.

[5] The income from a bond for any dividend period is found by multiplying the book value as of the beginning of the period by the yield originally purchased. It is assumed for present purposes that dividends are paid and interest is compounded annually. The annual incomes from a single tax-exempt investment equal $Y_e P_1, Y_e P_2, \cdots, Y_e P_n$, where $P_1, P_2, \cdots, P_n$ represent book values of the investment at the beginning of the successive years (or dividend periods) during which it is held.

$$P_1 = R - R(Y_e - C)a_{\overline{n}|Y_e}, \qquad P_2 = R - R(Y_e - C)a_{\overline{n-1}|Y_e}, \cdots,$$

$$P_n = R - R(Y_e - C)a_{\overline{n-(n-1)}|Y_e}.$$

Looking at the matter from another angle, in bonds purchased at a premium, the book value is reduced each dividend period by the difference between the dividend and the return, based on the yield originally purchased, on the book value of the bonds at the beginning of the period. Hence, P_1 = the purchase price, $P_2 = P_1 - (RC - Y_e P_1)$, $P_3 = P_2 - (RC - Y_e P_2)$, etc. Conversely, with bonds purchased at a discount, the book value is increased during each period by the difference between the return on the book value of the bond and the dividend, that is, $P_2 = P_1 + (Y_e P_1 - RC)$, etc.

[6] The investment-in-exemption equals

$$DP_1(1 + Y_t)^{-1} + DP_2(1 + Y_t)^{-2} + \cdots + DP_n(1 + Y_t)^{-n} = \sum_{i=1}^{n} DP_i(1 + Y)^{-i}$$

The formula can easily be modified to apply to the usual case where dividends are paid and interest is compounded semiannually.

In tax-exempt bonds bought at par, the investment-in-exemption might also be regarded, although less usefully, as the difference between the price of the bonds bought tax exempt and their price if they were bought to be taxable. It can be shown that the amount of the investment-in-exemption so defined is the same as the amount given by the above formula.

[7] Assuming that dividends are paid and interest is compounded annually.

[8] The gross tax saving = $T_{ti}(Y_t P_i)$. See pp. 140–141, n. 1, for the meaning of the notation and a discussion of the concept of the marginal tax rate.

[9] *Internal Revenue Code*, Sec. 117 (f).

[10] 282 U. S. 216 (1931).

[11] G.C.M. 10452, XI-1 C.B. 18; see also *Moody's Investment Manual, Municipals 1948*, p. A 27. Laws of most states prohibit issuance of municipal securities at discounts.

[12] I.R.C., Sec. 125.

[13] *Ibid.*

[14] Let the tax so computed be designated by gT. Then for any given year i the gross tax saving equals $T_{ti}(Y_t P_i) - gT_i$.

[15] Net tax saving equals:

$T_{ti}(Y_t P_i) - DP_i$, or, if the tax-exempt bonds were purchased at a taxable discount, $T_{ti}(Y_t P_i) - gT_i - DP_i$. (See pp. 140–141, n. 1, for the meaning of the notation used.)

[16] It is assumed that the bonds originally were issued at par or above.

[17] Let S represent the gross tax savings realized in any year (equals $T_t(Y_tP)$ or $T_t(Y_tP)$ $- gT$). See p. 142, nn. 8, 14.

The accumulated value of gross tax savings for n years equals

$$S_1(1+r)^{n-1} + S_2(1+r)^{n-2} + \cdots + S_n, \quad \text{or} \quad \sum_{i=1}^{n} S_i(1+r)^{n-i}$$

For bondholders who bought tax-exempt bonds at a premium before 1942, this amount is increased by the tax saving made possible by the fact that the premium amortized before 1942 can be claimed as a capital loss when the bonds are redeemed.

Let A represent the income sacrificed in any year (equals DP). At the time of redemption, the accumulated value of income sacrificed equals:

$$\sum_{i=1}^{n} A_i(1+r)^{n-i}$$

The interest rate r represents the yields at which the successive gross tax savings or income increments could have been invested. If the value of r changes over the period, as it probably does in most cases, the formulas should be modified accordingly. For present purposes, however, changes in the value of r can be ignored, since they would affect S and A alike.

[18] If the bonds had been bought at a discount (assuming they were originally issued at par or above), the taxable capital gain would be the difference between the original cost to the bondholder and the sales price. In bonds originally issued at a discount, this amount is reduced by the proportion of the issuing discount amortized during the time they are held by the bondholder. (See pp. 34–35.)

[19] The reader may ask why A's alternative gain or loss should not be computed upon 1,000 taxable bonds, since his original alternative was to purchase that number. The reason is that in effect $8.75 of the principal originally invested in tax exempts was disinvested at the book value; to compare the tax exempt with the hypothetical taxable situation, a corresponding disinvestment, at book value, must be assumed for the latter.

[20] Assume a single investment in tax-exempt bonds is sold at the end of year j.

Let jS = the accumulated value of gross tax savings from the time of purchase to the time of sale.

jA = the accumulated value of the income sacrificed from the time of purchase to the time of sale.

P_{eb} = the book value at the end of j of the tax-exempt investment.

P_{em} = the market value at the end of j of the tax-exempt investment.

P_{tb} = the book value at the end of j of comparable taxable bonds ($= P_{eb}$).

P_{tm} = the market value at the end of j of comparable taxable bonds whose book value is P_{tb}.

T_g = the capital gains tax rate to which the bondholder will be subject.

The relative capital gain or loss resulting from the sale of the tax-exempt bonds equals

$$(P_{em} - P_{eb}) - (P_{tm} - P_{tb}), \quad \text{which equals} \quad P_{em} - P_{tm}.$$

The total gain or loss from investing in tax exempts instead of comparable taxables equals

$$jS - jA + (P_{em} - P_{tm})(1 - T_g).$$

Note: This formula may be slightly inaccurate in some cases, since it is assumed that the value of T_g is the same for the capital gain or loss arising from the sale of tax exempts and the gain or loss arising from the sale of comparable taxables. If the difference between these two magnitudes is large, the values of T_g applicable to each may be different.

[21] Municipal Finance Officer's Association, Committee on Municipal Debt Administration, *The Call Feature in Municipal Bonds* (Chicago: 1938).

[22] At the present time, bondholders who have bought bonds at a premium are required to amortize the premium to the earliest call date (no amortization is allowed where the call date is indefinite, e.g., on 30 days notice). If bonds are not redeemed at the earliest redemption date the bondholder may continue writing off any unamortized part of the premium originally paid (with tax-exempt bonds this applies only to bonds purchased before 1942). (See Treasury *Regulations 111*, Sec. 29.125-1 to 29.125-9.)

Callable bonds are ordinarily sold at a slightly higher yield than noncallable bonds comparable in risk and maturity; sometimes bond contracts carry a provision for the payment of a premium if the bonds are called before maturity.

[23] "Here, at last, is a 'commodity' with respect to which the tradition and naïve conception of 'consumer surplus' has clear meaning and significance . . . And it is precisely this 'consumer surplus' which reflects the folly of the exemption." Henry Simons, *Personal Income Taxation* (Chicago: University of Chicago Press, 1938), pp. 173–174.

[24] K. E. Boulding, "The Concept of Economic Surplus," *American Economic Review* (December, 1945), p. 851.

[25] State and local governments might capitalize on this inelastic demand of certain groups for municipal bonds even if exemption did not exist if they could employ the discriminating monopolist's tactic of charging higher prices to buyers with more inelastic demands. (The federal government resorted to this practice in financing the recent war in restricting the marketability of some issues and specifying who could be the holders.) The existence of the yield differential arising out of exemption has made such exploitation possible without differentiating in the market prices of securities and in a way which does not involve the necessity of isolating the buyers with the more inelastic demands.

[26] The principal attempts to compute an aggregate gain or loss are those by C. O. Hardy, *Tax-Exempt Securities and the Surtax;* H. L. Lutz, *The Fiscal and Economic Effects of the Taxation of Public Securities, a Report Prepared for the Comptroller of the State of New York* (privately printed, also printed in the *Hearings before the Special [Senate] Committee . . . ,* 1939, pp. 91–186); and the Treasury department at various times, for example, *Hearings before the Special [Senate] Committee,* 1939, pp. 573–604.

These studies have employed the technique of assuming an average differential for all outstanding securities and then computing the increased cost to states and localities if they had originally floated all their outstanding loans at the original cost increased by this assumed differential.

The procedure is irrelevant to the question of the current advantage to states and localities arising out of the existence of tax exemption in the past, since the differentials involved are those assumed to exist at a given time, and it is usually recognized as irrelevant. But it is also irrelevant to the question of the ultimate gains or losses from abolishing exemption, since it involves the assumption that other things, including bond yields and tax rates, remain the same for as much as forty or fifty years.

Notes   145

Hardy and Lutz concluded that exemption probably benefits all governments on net balance; the Treasury calculations have indicated that the exemption involves a net loss. Although the Treasury calculations are more carefully handled than those of either Hardy or Lutz, they cannot mean much because of the basic shortcomings of the technique.

[27] Simons, *op. cit.*, p. 157.

[28] *Ibid.*, p. 177.

[29] The suggestion has been made that states and localities exploit the differential between taxable federal bonds and nontaxable municipals by selling large amounts of municipals and investing part of the proceeds in higher yield federal bonds; thus allowing the municipal obligation to be carried free of charge. (See, for example, I. M. Labovitz, "Aftermath of War in State Finance," *Proceedings, National Tax Association,* 1946, pp. 67–68.) If this plan were widely adopted, the differential probably would be wiped out in short order.

NOTES TO CHAPTER IV

[1] See Hardy, *op. cit.*, for an excellent discussion of the issues raised.

[2] Simons, *op. cit.*, p. 172.

[3] *Ibid.*, p. 176.

[4] Simons: "The whole policy of exemption works out like a subsidy distributed in the form of relief from surtaxes and financed by levies upon small savers." *Ibid.*, p. 177.

[5] Probably this is true only to the extent that federal taxes are reduced by subsidies to wealthy bondholders. See chap. v.

[6] The Treasury estimated in 1939 that at that time approximately $7 billion of municipals (including obligations of territories and possessions) were held by individuals with net incomes of $5,000 and over. *Tax-Exempt Securities, Hearings Before the Committee on Ways and Means,* House of Representatives, 76th Cong., 1 sess., 1939, p. 37.

[7] See, for example, the protest of the National Educational Association, *Hearings Before the Committee on Ways and Means on Revenue Revision of 1942,* House of Representatives, 77th Cong., 2 sess., 1942, pp. 1599–1600.

[8] Principally statistics which show that tax-exempt securities have constituted only a relatively small percentage of the assets in large estates. See Lutz, *op. cit.*, pp. 45–51 and Appendix D. It is notable, however, that the holdings of tax exempts have been relatively largest in the largest estates. See the Treasury's estimates, *Hearings before the Committee on Ways and Means,* 1942, p. 3087.

[9] Simons, *op. cit.*, p. 175. (Author's italics).

[10] See, for example, Hardy, *op. cit.*, chap. iii; Powell, *op. cit.*, pp. 58–66; Robert Murray Haig, testimony before the Tax Court in the Shamberg Case, pp. 1350–1357.

[11] B. U. Ratchford says: "There are no complete data on the interest and principal payments which states make on account of their debts. However, such data as are available indicate that such payments were heavier in the Southeast than in any other region, both in relation to the revenue receipts of the states and in relation to the income of taxpayers. This was true despite the fact that southern states were making smaller payments on principal than were other states." *American State Debts* (Durham: Duke University Press, 1941), p. 540.

In 1940, six of the nine states having the highest ratio of state and local gross debt per capita to economic income per capita were in the low-income southeast. (A breakdown by states of postwar state and local debt was not available at the time of this writing.)

States	Per cent per capita debt of per capita income
Arkansas	45.4
Florida	50.2
Louisiana	48.1
Mississippi	42.1
New Jersey	45.5
New Mexico	40.8
New York	48.1
North Carolina	43.1
Tennessee	48.7

SOURCE: Bureau of the Census, *State and Local Government Debt:* 1940 (State and Local Government Special Study No. 13), data selected from Table 19, p. 35.

[12] Hardy, *op. cit.*, chap. ii; also Powell, *op. cit.*, chap. iv.

[13] *Cong. Record.* 73d Cong., 1 sess., 1933, pp. 5420–5421. For a more extensive discussion of the agitation during this period, see Derrick, *op. cit.*, pp. 23–33.

[14] *Cong. Record*, 1933, p. 5857.

[15] *United States News*, June 24, 1935, p. 16.

[16] *Hearings Before the Special [Senate] Committee*, 1939, p. 2. The most important of the decisions referred to was Helvering v. Gerhardt, 304 U. S. 405 (1938).

[17] *Hearings Before the Special [Senate] Committee*, 1939, p. 2.

[18] *Hearings Before the Committee on Ways and Means*, 1939.

[19] *Hearings Before the Special [Senate] Committee*, 1939.

[20] *Hearings Before the Ways and Means Committee*, 1939.

[21] See the statement of Senator Prentice Brown, *Cong. Record*, 76th Cong., 3 sess., 1940, p. 12291.

[22] *Ibid.*, p. 12304.

[23] *Wall Street Journal*, January 24, 1941, p. 1.

[24] *Ibid.*, February 28, 1941, p. 1.

[25] *Hearings before the Ways and Means and Senate Finance Committees*, on the revenue revision of 1942.

[26] H. R. 7378.

[27] *Cong. Record*, 77th Cong., 2 sess., 1942, p. 7949.

[28] Early in 1939, the Gallup Poll showed that 75 per cent of the public polled favored abolishing the exemption. Senator Brown, Chairman of the Special Senate Committee, who had charge of the bill abolishing exemption in 1940, said that out of more than 700 newspaper editorials published on the subject, 64 per cent favored immediate removal, 14 per cent suggested a constitutional amendment, and only 9 per cent were opposed. (*Washington Post*, February 8, 1939.)

[29] Henry Epstein, "Aspects of Tax Exemption of Municipals," *Commercial and Financial Chronicle*, March 1, 1945, pp. 933, 936.

NOTES TO CHAPTER V

[1] Discussion of income magnitudes may seem somewhat pathetic because of the relative smallness of the income flows arising directly out of state and local bond interest transfers. On the same grounds, however, the whole problem of state and local bond taxation might be dismissed. Moreover, recent business-cycle theory demonstrates that income fluctua-

tions furnish an excellent demonstration of the proverb that great oaks from little acorns grow, in this case through the operation of the consumption multiplier and the acceleration principle. The point is that income effects, however small they may be with relation to total income, are nevertheless important to this problem.

[2] The arguments for abolishing state and local immunity apply with equal force to the immunity of federal bonds from (nondiscriminatory) state income taxation, so that any reform program should include the abolition of this federal immunity. Thus the extent to which the disadvantages to the states and localities would be mitigated by the income from taxing federal bond interest should also be considered. This is discussed at a later point (see chap. vi).

[3] This is demonstrated by the following table of revenues of states and localities for 1947:

Per Cent Distribution of State and Local Government Revenue by Source, 1947

Taxes	81.9
Individual income	3.0
Corporate income	3.0
Sales, use and gross receipts	24.4
Property	36.0
Death and gift	1.1
Social insurance	6.3
Licenses, permits, and other	8.1
Charges and miscellaneous	10.5
Aid received from federal government	7.6

SOURCE: Bureau of the Census, *Governmental Revenue in 1947*, August, 1948, p. 9. Total state and local government revenue in 1947 estimated at $15.3 billions.

[4] In 1947, approximately 90 per cent of local government tax revenue came from this source. *Ibid.*

[5] See Haig's testimony in the Shamberg case. In 1947, approximately 28 per cent of local government revenues came from other governments, principally from the states. Bureau of the Census, *Governmental Revenue in 1947*, loc. cit.

[6] Bureau of the Census, *State Tax Collections in 1948*, August, 1948; also Frederick A. Peitzsch, "New Sources of Municipal Revenue in 1947," *Municipal Year Book, 1948*, pp. 176–192.

[7] Some economists would disagree with this point and would maintain that the effects upon equity of this type of adjustment would be favorable rather than unfavorable on the grounds that the users of the service or good would pay a price that represented the full cost of its use, whereas if revenue bonds are exempted from taxation part of the cost of the service or good is subsidized by the federal government and ultimately by taxpayers other than the users. (For example, see Haig's testimony in the Shamberg case.)

Assume that the problem concerns a bridge for which revenue bonds have been issued. Analysis can start with the proposition that the optimum use of the bridge will be established at the price which equates demand with marginal cost (providing the demand at this price does not exceed the capacity of the bridge), since up to this point it will be socially beneficial to divert resources from other employments and put them to work operating the bridge. (See Harold Hotelling, "The General Welfare in Relation to Problems of Taxation and of Railway and Utility Rates," *Econometrica* [1938], pp. 242–269.)

Since the average cost for revenue-producing projects (like bridges and tunnels) is likely to be decreasing in the range of output at which the price is set, owing to the high proportion of fixed to variable charges, the marginal cost is likely to be less than the average cost at the point of optimum use. If this is so, there will have to be a subsidy to make up the difference between average and marginal cost.

The traditional test of the economy of the bridge (i.e., whether its building constituted a wise use of resources) is whether the revenue from the sale of its products or services covers all costs. This argument is rejected by the welfare economic analysis on the grounds that the community's choice of the use of available resources should be based upon the benefit derived from the optimum use of possible projects, and that this optimum use ordinarily will not be attained unless the price is set at the marginal cost. (Hotelling, *op. cit.*, pp. 267–268.)

If the demand for the use of the bridge is highly inelastic, the price can be raised from marginal to average cost without markedly decreasing its use. In this case the subsidy (the difference between average and marginal cost) is paid by those who use the bridge and the problem is simply one of whether it is more desirable to collect the subsidy from them or from someone else, income taxpayers, for example. An argument can be made, on the basis of the benefit principle, for "taxing" the bridge users by charging them a price equal to average cost.

But if the demand for the service or good is elastic, which seems a plausible assumption for many public projects (e.g., the George Washington Bridge at New York City, which competes with tunnels, ferries, and bridges further upstream), the analysis is not so simple. Raising the price from marginal to average cost will decrease the use of the bridge much below the optimum point; at the same time, the average cost will be higher than at the optimum point. Here the ramifications of the problem extend far beyond the question of whether the bridge users or someone else should pay the difference between marginal and average cost at the point of optimum use.

Finally, the above analysis, strictly speaking, applies only if constructing the bridge diverted resources away from other employments. If the resources used in its construction otherwise would have been unemployed, there is no question of alternative cost and hence of fixed cost, at least from the standpoint of the whole economy.

If the demand for the services or goods produced by a revenue-producing project is elastic, the only instance in which an increase in the price of such services or goods (relative to what otherwise would be the case) might be economically beneficial is the case in which the price otherwise would be set below marginal cost. But to the extent that abolishing exemption would cause the price to be raised above marginal cost, use of the project would be reduced below the optimum point.

[8] It may be argued, however, that the present system has the effect of reducing state and local taxes by decreasing federal expenditures, and that this is not a very efficient system either.

[9] This would apply to individual bondholders and to institutions other than commercial banks. It might apply also to commercial banks if their total lending capacity were the same in both cases and if they tended to lend to capacity. But in so far as foregone holdings of federal bonds were not replaced by other investments, the effect would be to reduce total deposits and hence to counteract inflationary tendencies. If the proportion of municipals held by commercial banks should be no greater in the future than in the past, however, the effect would be small in any case. (See the *Annual Report of the Secretary of the Treasury*, 1946, p. 672.)

[10] William C. Beyer, "Financial Dictators Replace Political Boss," *National Municipal Review* (April, 1933), pp. 162–167.

[11] See J. M. Clark, *Economics of Planning Public Works* (Washington: Federal Emergency Administration of Public Works, 1935), pp. 105 ff.

[12] See Hardy, *op. cit.*

[13] For example, see the statement of the Under Secretary of the Treasury, John W. Hanes, *Hearings before the Committee on Ways and Means*, 1939, pp. 452–454; and James C. Bonbright's testimony before the Tax Court in the Shamberg case.

[14] See the *Hearings before the Special [Senate] Committee* and the *Committee on Ways and Means*, 1939; and the Senate and House *Hearings* on the revenue bill of 1942; also the Petitioner's evidence in the Shamberg case, which was directed principally at proving that taxing bond interest would materially impede state and local financing. Carl H. Chatters, executive director of the Municipal Finance Officers Association, pointed out that abolishing exemption would (a) push marginal debtors beyond their economic ability to pay, (b) push others beyond their legal interest limit, and (c) cause some bonds to become unattractive because the added cost of debt service would strain the financial capacities of the issuing jurisdictions; he emphasized also that these effects would be exacerbated during depressions. (*Ibid.*, p. 691.)

[15] See Carl H. Chatters, "Constitutional Tax Restrictions on Local Government Finance," *Proceedings, National Tax Association*, 1944, pp. 342–349; also George Spicer, "Fiscal Aspects of State-Local Relations," *The Annals* (January, 1940), pp. 151–160, and references there cited. A number of states have recently undertaken to guarantee loans contracted by local agencies to finance housing. Dorothy Gazzolo, "Housing Developments in 1947," *Municipal Year Book, 1948*, p. 284.

[16] Of course, the mere fact that state and local government expenditures may create employment is not of itself an argument for granting tax exemption privileges only to state and local governments during periods of unemployment. If lowering interest rates to borrowers generally (e.g., through tax exemption) will promote employment, then there is an argument for lowering them to everyone, and if state and local governments are to be granted special favors, it should be for some other reason than to stimulate employment.

[17] See, for example, Alvin Hansen and Harvey Perloff, *State and Local Finance in the National Economy* (New York: W. W. Norton & Co., 1944), pp. 213–218; also Louis Shere, "Tax Reserves for State and Local Governments," *Proceedings, National Tax Association*, 1945, pp. 187–199. To be effective as a countercylical device, as Hansen and Perloff point out, the funds should be sterilized in good times, perhaps by putting them into dormant bank deposits.

[18] Ambrose Fuller, *Legislative Authorization for the Creation of Capital Reserves for Future Municipal Outlays*, Memorandum prepared for the American Municipal Association, Series AM, No. 26 (July, 1942), cited in Hansen and Perloff, *op. cit.*, p. 215.

[19] Fuller, *op. cit.*, p. 6.

[20] It is true that the states as a whole are coming to rely more heavily upon the income tax. In 1947, however, personal income taxes accounted for only 3 per cent of total state and local revenue, and personal and corporation taxes together accounted for only 6 per cent (above, p. 147, n. 3).

[21] See Paul Studenski, *Measurement of Variations in State Economic and Fiscal Capacity*, Bureau Memorandum No. 50, Federal Security Agency, Social Security Board, Bureau of Research and Statistics, Washington, D.C., 1943; also J. Wilner Sundelson and S. J. Muskin, *The Measurement of State and Local Tax Effort*, Bureau Memorandum No. 58,

1944. Studenski concludes that an index comprising anuual figures for per capita income produced and per capita income received would be the most satisfactory index of the economic and fiscal capacity of states.

NOTES TO CHAPTER VI

[1] At the present time, federal bond interest income of corporations is taxed by a number of states through corporation excise taxes, under the legal fiction that such income is a part of the measure, but not the subject, of the tax. The Supreme Court has upheld the authority of the states to levy such taxes in Pacific Co. *v.* Johnson, 285 U. S. 480; and Educational Films Co. *v.* Ward, 282 U. S. 379.

[2] See the Treasury memorandum prepared for the Special Senate Committee, 1939, *Hearings*, pp. 638–639.

[3] See the comments of Carl H. Chatters before the Special Senate Committee, 1939, *Hearings*, p. 387.

[4] It is questionable, of course, whether some bondholders currently nontaxable should be permitted to continue enjoying this privilege.

[5] See Henry J. Bittermann, *State and Federal Grants-in-Aid* (Chicago: Mentzer, Bush & Co., 1938); Raymond Uhl and A. V. Shea, "State Administered and Locally-Shared Taxes," *Municipal Year Book, 1936*; Treasury Committee on Intergovernmental Fiscal Relations, *Federal, State and Local Government Fiscal Relations* (Senate Document No. 69, 78th Cong., 1 sess. 1943). By the end of 1947, only four states did not provide for sharing state-collected taxes or for making grants-in-aid to other governmental units of the state. H. G. Pope, "Our Cities in 1947," *Municipal Year Book, 1948*, p. 4.

NOTES TO CHAPTER VII

[1] In considering how to tax "present" holders and future buyers of securities outstanding at the time the tax is introduced, states and localities can be ignored, since they will be affected only by the taxation of new or refunding securities issued subsequent to the introduction of the tax.

[2] Some proposals have been devised principally with a view of getting around presumed constitutional obstacles to outright exemption. See pp. 108–110.

[3] See the *Hearings* on the 1942 revenue bill before the Ways and Means and Senate Finance Committees.

[4] See, for example, the colloquy between Randolph Paul and Representative Frank Buck, *Hearings before the Committee on Ways and Means*, pp. 3110–3114.

[5] A classic case is that of the loss to brewers and distillers imposed by the eighteenth amendment.

[6] Assume that exemption is abolished as of the end of year k. Before exemption is abolished, the annual gross tax saving of any given year i equals $T_{ti}(Y_tP_i)$, or in case the tax-exempt securities were originally purchased at a taxable discount, $T_{ti}(Y_tP_i) - gT_i$. (Note: See above, pp. 140–141, n. 1, for definitions of the notation used and pp. 140 ff., for a discussion of the derivation of these formulas.)

After exemption is abolished, the bondholder pays a tax on his previously exempt income equal to $T_e(Y_eP)$, where T_e equals the marginal tax rate applicable to such income. The gross tax saving for any given year is thus reduced to $T_{ti}(Y_tP_i) - T_{ei}(Y_eP_i)$, or, for bonds purchased at a taxable discount, $T_{ti}(Y_tP_i) - gT_i - T_{ti}C$, writing C for the bond coupon.

Let the annual gross tax savings before abolition be designated by S and annual gross tax savings after abolition by s. Then if exemption is abolished at the end of year k, the accumulated value of the gross tax savings at the time of redemption would be

$$\sum_{i=1}^{k} S_i(1+r)^{n-i} + \sum_{i=k}^{n} s_i(1+r)^{n-i}.$$

Let the accumulated value as of the redemption date of the investment-in-exemption be represented by nA, the corresponding accumulated value of gross tax savings realized before abolition by nkS, and the accumulated value of gross tax savings realized after abolition by ks.

Then if $nA \leqq (nkS + ks)$, the bondholder, having amortized the entire value of his investment-in-exemption, cannot claim to have suffered an "undue" capital loss by this criterion, since he is at least as well off as if he bought comparable taxable bonds.

[7] Let nS equal the value of gross tax savings, assuming exemption had *not* been abolished, accumulated to the date of redemption. Then the "undue" loss equals

$$nA - (nkS + ks), \qquad \text{or where} \qquad nS < nA,$$
$$nS - (nkS + ks).$$

[8] Assume that the bonds representing a single investment are sold in year j. As before, let

jS = the hypothetical accumulated value of gross tax savings from purchase to sale, assuming (contrary to fact) that exemption were maintained.

jkS = the accumulated value at the time of sale of gross tax savings realized before the abolition of exemption.

ks = the accumulated value at the time of sale of gross tax savings realized after abolition of exemption.

jA = the accumulated value of the income sacrificed from purchase to sale by buying tax exempts.

P_{eb} = the book value at the time of sale of the bonds originally bought to be tax exempt.

P_{em} = the hypothetical market value of these bonds at the time of sale assuming (contrary to fact) that exemption were maintained.

P_{et} = the amount received for the previously tax-exempt bonds.

P_{tm} = the hypothetical market value as of the sale date of comparable taxable bonds the book value of which is P_{ec}.

T_g = the capital gains tax rate to which the bondseller is subject.

The net relative gain or loss from an operation in tax exempts where exemption is maintained (see above, pp. 143–144, n. 20) equals

$$jS - jA + (P_{em} - P_{tm})(1 - T_g).$$

If exemption is abolished, the bondholder suffers a diminution of gross tax savings equal to $jS - (jkS + ks)$ and a capital loss equal to $(P_{em} - P_{et})(1 - T_g)$. But since there is no real value for P_{em} this capital loss is only of theoretical interest.

The net relative gain or loss from the operation in tax exempts equals

$$jS - jA + (P_{em} - P_{tm})(1 - T_g) - [jS - (jkS + ks)] - (P_{em} - P_{et})(1 - Tg)$$

which simplifies to

$$(jkS + ks) - jA - (P_{tm} - P_{et})(1 - T_g).$$

In the simplified version the troublesome term P_{em} disappears and all the remaining terms are determinable or can be estimated with a fair degree of accuracy, so that the net gain or loss from the whole operation in (originally) tax-exempt securities can be determined approximately. Without knowing the value of the bonds to sell tax exempt, however, it is impossible to determine how much of the net relative gain or loss from operating in tax exempts is due to the abolition of exemption. "Undue" capital losses can be estimated for policy purposes, therefore, only on the basis of arbitrary assumptions.

[9] Rigorous application of the principle would require not only that the subsidies of supramarginal bondholders be confiscated but also that the losses of submarginal holders be restored. This is discussed on pp. 91–92.

[10] Since the tax is equal to the subsidy, the general formula for the tax is the same as for the subsidy (see above, p. 140 ff.). As before, let

P = the book value of a single investment as of the beginning of a dividend period. To simplify the following discussion, it is assumed that the dividend period, like the tax period, is one year and that the beginning of the dividend period coincides with the beginning of the tax period. The formula can easily be modified to take care of the usual situation where interest is paid semiannually.

In any case, the value of P is ascertainable from the bondholder's books.

Y_e = the effective yield originally purchased.

Y_t = the yield obtainable at the time of the original investment on comparable taxable securities.

$D = Y_t - Y_e$ = the differential between the tax-exempt and taxable yields prevailing at the time of the original investment.

T_t = the tax rate which would currently apply to an income, incremental to the bondholder's ordinary taxable income, equal to the sum of the incomes from all the bondholder's single investments in municipals increased by the differentials allowed for computing the tax.

The tax on the income from a single investment equals

$$a) \quad T_t(Y_tP) - DP$$
$$b) \quad = T_t(Y_eP + DP) - DP$$
$$c) \quad = T_t(Y_eP) - (1 - T_t)DP$$

Note: To limit the application of the tax to supramarginal bondholders a provision should be included that the allowable credit (DP) should not exceed the gross tax $T_t(Y_tP)$.

Some modifications may need to be introduced for bonds bought at a discount (see text above, p. 90). The tax formula would be $T_t(1 + D_e)C - CD_e$ (writing C for the bond dividend and D_e for D/Y_e).

It should be emphasized that this is a tax at preferential rates upon previously tax-exempt income and not upon hypothetical income. The same formula is mentioned in the report of the Treasury Committee on Intergovernmental Fiscal Relations, where it is described as follows: ". . . a proposal to allow the taxpayer a credit against taxes roughly equivalent to the differential caused by tax exemption. If this credit were, in addition, subject to inclusion in the taxpayer's income for tax purposes . . . the differential advantage of large taxpayers would be wiped out." (*Op. cit.*, p. 306.)

From still another point of view, suggested by the formula as written in (c) above, the effect is that of (1) a gross tax upon the municipal bond income, minus (2) a credit equal to income *after tax* sacrificed by having bought tax-exempt instead of taxable securities.

[11] Notably the mutual savings banks. Unfortunately, there are no data on the shifts of holdings of private individuals. (See the *Annual Report of the Secretary of the Treasury*, 1946, p. 672.)

[12] This point might be used to support the argument that refunds should be made to submarginal holders, since it is possible that refunds would cost the federal government relatively little.

[13] See chap. ii, above.

[14] See chap. ii, above.

[15] Write C_r for the fixed relative differential. The rate of the tax is $T_t - (1 - T_t)C_r$.

[16] See pp. 151–152, n. 8, for a detailed analysis of the gain or loss accruing to bondholders who sell their bonds after the abolition of exemption.

[17] It has been shown (p. 151, n. 8) that if exemption were completely abolished, liquidating bondholders would suffer a dimunition of gross tax savings plus a capital loss (before tax credit) equal to $P_{em} - P_{et}$, where P_{em} is the hypothetical market value of the bonds, at the time of the sale, assuming (contrary to fact) that full exemption were maintained, and P_{et} is the selling price of the same bonds to be fully taxable. In effect, the *frd* plan gives every present bondholder who sells his bonds before redemption an amount equal to the capital loss so defined, P_{em} being determined arbitrarily by the value of C_r.

[18] The marginal tax bracket would be defined by $C_r/(1 + C_r)$; if $C_r = 1.00$, for example, the marginal tax bracket would be 50 per cent, etc.

[19] It was recommended in connection with "model" tax on present holders that the credit allowed should not exceed the gross tax, so that present submarginal holders would be as well off as if no tax had been levied but not so well off as if they had originally bought taxables. (See pp. 92–93.)

[20] Under this plan, some individuals who owned bonds at the time of inauguration of the new tax plan and subsequently acquired more bonds of outstanding issues might have to segregate the credit allowed on the future purchases from that allowed on present holdings, since the former would be deductible from the tax liability on ordinary income whereas the latter would not. This would complicate the computation but should raise no essential difficulties.

[21] *Agenda for Progressive Taxation* (New York: Ronald Press, 1947), pp. 53–55.

[22] Write T_e for the income tax rate applicable to the bondholder's municipal bond income, and T_m for the tax rate in the "break-even" tax bracket. The rate of the tax is $T_e - T_m$.

NOTES TO CHAPTER VIII

[1] *Proceedings, National Tax Association*, 1937, pp. 388–399.

[2] *Annual Report of the Secretary of the Treasury*, 1919, p. 24. Both the Glass and Magill proposals were devised primarily with a view of getting around constitutional obstacles and the latter, at least, was inspired by the Supreme Court's decision in Maxwell v. Bubgee, 250 U.S. 525 (1919). That decision permitted the State of New Jersey to tax the value of the part of a decedent's estate under the jurisdiction of New Jersey at rates determined by the size of the entire estate.

[3] Most of these suggestions were taken from an unpublished collection made available to the writer.

[4] This suggestion was made in 1922 to the Ways and Means Committee (see the *Hearings before the Committee on Ways and Means on Tax-Exempt Securities*, House of Representatives, 67th Cong., 2 sess., 1922.) Professor Edwin R. Seligman was asked to comment upon the suggestion, and made an unfavorable report in a letter to the Committee, February 13, 1922 (*ibid.*, pp. 114–116).

NOTES TO CHAPTER IX

[1] For example, the indebtedness of New York City, in 1946, amounted to approximately 16 per cent of the total state and local debt. At the same time the condition of New York City finances, owing partly to the perennial conflict between the city and state governments, is precarious. It is quite unlikely that such a proposal would be acceptable to either the state or the city.

[2] *Proceedings, National Tax Association*, 1941, p. 195.

[3] *Ibid.*

[4] Suggestions like that of the Treasury Department Committee on Intergovernmental Fiscal Relations, for payments from the federal government to the states and localities which would be a fixed percentage of the principal (as opposed to a fixed percentage of the interest cost) would involve an undue advantage to issuers of short-term and high-grade securities and a corresponding disadvantage to long-term and low-grade securities. (*Federal, State and Local Government Fiscal Relations*, p. 306.)

[5] *Op. cit.*

[6] Treasury Committee on Intergovernmental Fiscal Relations, *op. cit.*, p. 306.

[7] *Ibid.*

[8] *Ibid.*

[9] See Hansen and Perloff, *op. cit.*, p. 200.

[10] Wylie Kilpatrick, *State Supervision of Local Finance*, cited in Hansen and Perloff, *op. cit.*, pp. 203 ff.

[11] In some states it might be possible to set up such funds with revenues gained through taxing federal bond interest.

[12] Ratchford, *op. cit.*, chap. xv.

[13] Hansen and Perloff, *op. cit.*, pp. 203–205.

[14] *Ibid.*, p. 204.

[15] *Ibid.*

[16] See, for example, the Department of Justice Study, *Taxation of Government Bondholders and Employees* (Washington, 1938) and six volumes of appendices thereto; and the reply by the Attorneys General of the States and Counsel for certain of their Municipal Subdivisions, *The Constitutional Immunity of State and Municipal Securities*, 1938.

[17] There are many studies of this question: See, for example, Powell, *op. cit.*; Everett H. Snedecker, "National Taxation of State Instrumentalities," *Rocky Mountain Law Review*, December, 1942, pp. 8–63; and Thomas Reed Powell, "The Waning of Intergovernmental Tax Immunities," *Harvard Law Review*, May, 1945, pp. 633–674; also the studies of the Department of Justice and Attorneys General, previously cited.

[18] *Hearings* before the Ways and Means and Senate Finance Committees on the revenue bill of 1942; also arguments in the Shamberg case.

[19] State of New York, et al. *v.* U.S., 326 U.S. 572 (1946). Forty-five other states joined New York as *amici curiae*.

[20] "The problem cannot escape issues that do not lend themselves to judgment by criteria and methods of reasoning that are within the professional training and special competence of judges. Indeed, the claim of implied immunity by States from federal taxation raises questions not wholly unlike provisions of the Constitution, such as that of Art. IV, Sec. 4, guaranteeing States a republican form of government . . . which this Court has deemed not within its duty to adjudicate." *Ibid.*, p. 314.

[21] Stone, Reed, Murphy, Burton.

[22] *Ibid.*, p. 316.

[23] 199 U.S. 437.

[24] *Loc. cit.*, pp. 318 ff.

BIBLIOGRAPHY

Bibliography

Note: Although there is a voluminous bibliography on the subject of tax exemption of state and local bonds, much of the material is repetitious and most relevant information can be found in a comparatively few sources. Particular reference should be made to the six appendices to the Department of Justice study, referred to below, which contain photostated copies of most of the important material on the historical and constitutional aspects of the question which was published before 1938, including complete copies of at least two books and excerpts from a number of others, excerpts from Congressional Hearings and Debates, and many periodical articles, as well as newspaper editorials. Also, comprehensive bibliographies have been compiled by the Division of Bibliography of the Library of Congress.

Consequently, it was felt that no purpose would be served by including an extensive bibliography here. The following list of publications is divided into two parts: first, a few basic sources which include most of the important material on the subject; second, a list of the other books, pamphlets, and articles which have been cited in the text.

BASIC SOURCES

BOOKS AND PAMPHLETS

THE ATTORNEYS GENERAL OF THE STATES AND COUNCIL FOR CERTAIN OF THEIR MUNICIPAL SUBDIVISIONS, *The Constitutional Immunity of State and Municipal Securities* (privately printed), 1938.

DEPARTMENT OF JUSTICE, *Taxation of Government Bondholders and Employees* (Washington: 1938); also six volumes of appendices. Of the latter, there are only a few sets existent; one repository being, of course, the Library of Congress.

DERRICK, LUCILE, "Exemption of Security Interest from Income Taxes in the United States, an Economic and Statistical Analysis" (Studies in Business Administration, Vol. XVI, No. 4), *The Journal of Business of the University of Chicago*, October, 1946, Part 2.

HARDY, C. O., *Tax-Exempt Securities and the Surtax* (New York: Macmillan Co., 1926). An early evaluation, including a statistical analysis of the gains and losses accruing from tax exemption.

MACAULAY, FREDERICK R., *The Movements of Interest Rates, Bond Yields and Stock Prices in the United States Since 1856* (New York: National Bureau of Economic Research, 1938).

POWELL, ALDEN A., *National Taxation of State Instrumentalities*, Illinois Studies in the Social Sciences, Vol. XX, No. 4 (Urbana: University of Illinois Press, 1936). An excellent historical and constitutional analysis; includes an extensive bibliography.

SENATE HEARINGS

Hearings Before the Committee on Finance on H.R. 7378, 77th Cong.,
2 sess., 1942.
*Hearings Before the Special Committee on Taxation of Governmental Se-
curities and Salaries,* 76th Cong., 1 sess., 1939.

HOUSE HEARINGS

*Hearings Before the Committee on Ways and Means on Revenue Revision
of 1942,* 77th Cong., 2 sess., 1942.
*Tax-Exempt Securities, Hearings Before the Committee on Ways and
Means,* 76th Cong., 1 sess., 1939.
*Hearings Before the Committee on Ways and Means on Tax-Exempt Se-
curities,* 67th Cong., 2 sess., 1922.

BIBLIOGRAPHIES

LIBRARY OF CONGRESS, Division of Bibliography, *List of References on
Tax Exemption of Securities* (mimeographed), 1922, supplement 1931,
supplement 1938.
BLAKEY, GLADYS C., "Important Publications on Public Finance
1940–4," *Proceedings, National Tax Association,* 1944, pp. 23–39.
BLAKEY, ROY G. and GLADYS C., "Recent Publications on Public Finance," *Proceedings, National Tax Association,* 1940, pp. 84–86.
CULVER, DOROTHY C., "A Bibliography of Intergovernmental Relations
in the United States," *The Annals,* January, 1940, pp. 210–218.

OTHER REFERENCES CITED IN TEXT
BOOKS AND PAMPHLETS

BITTERMANN, HENRY J., *State and Federal Grants-in-Aid* (Chicago:
Mentzer, Bush & Co., 1938).
BUREAU OF THE CENSUS, *State and Local Government Debt: 1940,* State
and Local Government Special Study No. 13.
———, *Governmental Revenue in 1947,* August, 1948.
———, *State Tax Collections in 1948,* August, 1948.
CLARK, J. M., *Economics of Planning Public Works* (Washington:
Federal Emergency Administration of Public Works, 1935).
COMMITTEE FOR ECONOMIC DEVELOPMENT, *A Postwar Tax Plan for High
Employment* (New York: 1944).
DURAND, DAVID, *Basic Yields of Corporate Bonds 1900-1942* (New York:
National Bureau of Economic Research, Technical Paper 3, 1942).

DURAND, DAVID, and WINN, WILLIS J., *Basic Yields of Bonds, 1926–1947: Their Measurement and Pattern* (New York: National Bureau of Economic Research, Technical Paper 6, 1947).

ELLIS, PAUL, *The World's Biggest Business* (New York: National Industrial Conference Board, 1944).

FULLER, AMBROSE, *Legislative Authorization for the Creation of Capital Reserves for Future Municipal Outlays*, Memorandum Prepared for the American Municipal Association, Series AM, No. 26 (July, 1942).

HANSEN, ALVIN, and PERLOFF, HARVEY, *State and Local Finance in the National Economy* (New York: W. W. Norton & Co., 1944).

HICKMAN, W. BRADDOCK, "The Term Structure of Interest Rates, An Exploratory Analysis" (New York: National Bureau of Economic Research, MS., November, 1942).

LUTZ, HARLEY L., *The Fiscal and Economic Effects of the Taxation of Public Securities, A Report Prepared for the Comptroller of the State of New York*, Privately printed, also printed in the *Hearings Before the Special [Senate] Committee on Taxation of Governmental Securities and Salaries*, U. S. Senate, 76th Cong., 1 sess., 1939, pp. 91–186.

MUNICIPAL FINANCE OFFICERS' ASSOCIATION, Committee on Municipal Debt Administration, *The Call Feature in Municipal Bonds* (Chicago: 1938).

MITCHELL, GEORGE W., LITTERER, OSCAR F., and DOMAR, EVSEY, "State and Local Finance," *Public Finance and Full Employment*, Postwar Economic Studies No. 3, Board of Governors of the Federal Reserve System (Washington: 1945).

RATCHFORD, B. U., *American State Debts* (Durham: Duke University Press, 1941).

RUML, BEARDSLEY, and SONNE, H. CHR., *Fiscal and Monetary Policy* (Washington: National Planning Association, 1944).

SIMONS, HENRY, *Personal Income Taxation* (Chicago: University of Chicago Press, 1938).

STANDARD STATISTICS COMPANY, *Standard Trade and Securities, Basic Statistics* (New York: 1936).

STUDENSKI, PAUL, *Measurement of Variations in State Economic and Fiscal Capacity*, Bureau Memorandum No. 50, Federal Security Agency, Social Security Board, Bureau of Research and Statistics (Washington: 1943).

SUNDELSON, J. WILNER, and MUSHKIN, S. J., *The Measurement of State and Local Tax Effort*, Bureau Memorandum No. 58, Federal Security Agency, Social Security Board, Bureau of Research and Statistics (Washington: 1944).

Treasury Committee on Intergovernmental Fiscal Relations, *Federal, State and Local Government Fiscal Relations*, Senate Document No. 69, 78th Cong., 1 sess., 1943.

Vickrey, William, *Agenda for Progressive Taxation* (New York: Ronald Press, 1947).

ARTICLES

Beyer, William C., "Financial Dictators Replace Political Boss," *National Municipal Review*, April, 1933, pp. 162–167.

Boulding, K. E., "The Concept of Economic Surplus," *American Economic Review*, December, 1945, pp. 851–869.

Chatters, Carl H., "Constitutional Tax Restrictions on Local Government Finance," *Proceedings, National Tax Association*, 1944, pp. 342–349.

Epstein, Henry, "Aspects of Tax Exemption of Municipals," *Commercial and Financial Chronicle*, March 1, 1945, pp. 933, 936.

Gazzolo, Dorothy, "Housing Developments in 1947," *Municipal Year Book, 1948*, pp. 278–287.

Hotelling, Harold, "The General Welfare in Relation to Problems of Taxation and of Railway and Utility Rates," *Econometrica*, 1938, pp. 242–269.

Labovitz, I. M., "Aftermath of War in State Finance," *Proceedings, National Tax Association*, 1946, pp. 57–69.

Lancaster, Lane, "State Limitations on Local Indebtedness," *Municipal Year Book, 1936*, pp. 313–327.

Magill, Roswell, "The Problem of Intergovernmental Tax Exemptions," *Proceedings, National Tax Association*, 1937, pp. 388–399.

Peitzsch, Frederick A., "New Sources of Municipal Revenue in 1947," *Municipal Year Book, 1948*, pp. 176–192.

Pope, H. G., "Our Cities in 1947," *Municipal Year Book, 1948*, pp. 1–7.

Powell, Thomas Reed, "The Waning of Intergovernmental Tax Immunities," *Harvard Law Review*, May, 1945, pp. 633–674.

Seltzer, Lawrence, "Possibilities of Speeding the Elimination of Tax Exempt Securities," *Proceedings, National Tax Association*, 1941, pp. 189–198.

Shere, Louis, "Tax Reserves for State and Local Governments," *Proceedings, National Tax Association*, 1945, pp. 187–199.

Snedecker, Everett H., "National Taxation of State Instrumentalities," *Rocky Mountain Law Review*, December, 1942, pp. 8–63.

SPICER, GEORGE, "Fiscal Aspects of State-Local Relations," *The Annals*, January, 1940, pp. 151–160.
UHL, RAYMOND, and SHEA, A. V., "State Administered and Locally-Shared Taxes," *Municipal Year Book, 1936*, pp. 367–389.

MISCELLANEOUS CITATIONS

PERIODICALS

The Bond Buyer, Survey of Current Business, Treasury Bulletin, United States News, Wall Street Journal.
Annual Report of the Secretary of the Treasury, 1919, 1946, 1948.
Commissioner *v.* Estate of Alexander Shamberg, Docket No. 107713 (1943), Tax Court of the United States; Testimony of James C. Bonbright, Carl Chatters, Harry Guthmann, Robert Murray Haig.

www.ingramcontent.com/pod-product-compliance
Lightning Source LLC
Chambersburg PA
CBHW021712210326
41599CB00013B/1627